Olivier Rœllinger's Contemporary French Cuisine

Fifty Recipes Inspired by the Sea

with Anne Testut and Alain Willaume

To the wind and the ocean, which, like fine food, bring people together.

The Spirit of Adventure

Olivier Rœllinger is half top chef, half corsair. He discovered his dual calling one dark night in the late 1970s in the delightful Breton port of Saint Malo, when he was set upon and severely injured in an unprovoked attack. This experience changed his life. He was forced to give up his studies in chemistry and bid farewell to his dream of sailing on all the world's oceans. Having learned the hard way that there are no certainties in life, that even the best-laid plans can be destroyed in an instant, he became an armchair traveler, visiting in his imagination all the places he had dreamed of seeing in real life. He was determined not to let the attack rule his life, however: remembering how as a child he had been fascinated by Saint Malo's maritime heritage, its links to the French East India Company, and the tales of piracy and swashbuckling adventure that were part of the town's history, he decided that he would relive their adventures in his own way. He read everything he could find about explorers and maritime heroes such as Jacques Cartier, Mahé de la Bourdonnais, Alain Gerbault, and Bernard Moitessier and decided to find a way to live the adventure he had dreamed of, despite the barriers fate had put in his way. Together with his wife, Jane, he found a way to bring the world and all its adventures to Saint Malo. His unquenchable enthusiasm for travel, meeting new people and discovering new places gave him the idea of becoming a kind of ambassador for the outstanding produce of his native region—an idea that, with his usual remarkable willpower, he rapidly put into practice.

Whatever Olivier Rœllinger undertakes, he brings to it his unbounded spirit of adventure and his deep love of the sea. These two passions are at the heart of everything he does, and give him his vital spark of creative energy. Having had time to reflect on the brevity of existence when ill health forced him to lead a sheltered life, he is always ready to set out on new ventures. He likes to compare himself to a sailor in a crow's nest, gazing out over the horizon, watching out for the land that will herald new adventures. In his own way, he has traveled all over the world and sailed all the oceans. The spices that arrive in his restaurant kitchen from all four corners of the globe whisper their secrets to him, and he listens to their tales.

The other major influence on Rœllinger's cuisine is the sea. Having grown up in a port with a fine maritime tradition, the sea is in his blood. He loves spending hours on the beach watching the ever-changing spectacle of the tide and the waves and dreaming of the distant lands across the ocean. Maybe that is why some of his closest friends are photographers. What he loves most about the sea is the feeling of being in the presence of something so vast, boundless, and timeless. Some people feel the same way about the desert, where there is nothing to interrupt the gaze as far as the horizon. Standing on the shore, listening to the keening of the wind, it is easy to understand how in centuries past people invented terrifying legends of sea monsters that would swallow ships whole. But Rœllinger has tamed the deep, harvesting its finest produce—delicious fleshy scallops, sea bass and other denizens of the sea; succulent Cancale oysters, Bouchot mussels, the tender young sole he ate as a child, and even the long fronds of seaweed that float lazily in the current.

Listening to Olivier Rœllinger talking about his love of the sea, it is obvious that this is what spurred him into taking up cooking. Like sailing, cooking is a way of exploring the world. The ocean is an invitation to a voyage. Cooking is a way of letting other people share the same fabulous adventure. Another thing both cooking and sailing have in common is that they are both the art of mastering the ephemeral—the splash and spray of the wake of the yacht disappears as surely as the carefully assembled ingredients in a lovingly crafted dessert. Again, both cause a sort of stage fright—the fear that vanishes as soon as the waves begin to slap the hull or the flames begin to hiss beneath the pan. And of course, for both, the conditions have to be right—the wind stiff but not a gale, the ingredients fresh and full of flavor. When the conditions are perfect, the result is pure exhilaration.

Rœllinger's love of the sea has served him well in his career. His love of traveling and his passion for fine food have won him friends all over the world. It is fascinating to listen to him talking about the history of the culinary tradition he knows best, French cuisine, and in particular the profound impact that the history of global exploration has had on the way people in the West eat. He firmly believes that if

French cuisine has widely been considered to be the finest in the world from the seventeenth century to the present day, it is because French chefs have always been curious to try new ingredients—strawberries, beans, cacao, cumin—and have succeeded in coming up with a range of unexpected and superb marriages between local ingredients and exotic imports, such as lamb and beans, fish and potatoes, or lobster and tomatoes.

Rœllinger has boundless admiration for the men who were brave enough to sail off beyond the limits of the known world, and who brought back a number of ingredients that we now take for granted. These men were the early ambassadors for bell peppers, pineapples, cloves, and artichokes. A number of these ingredients have become so familiar that we forget that, in centuries past, they were unknown, even thought to be dangerous—tomatoes, for instance, were once considered deadly poison. He finds real pleasure in recounting the tales of how these ingredients reached our tables—the war for supremacy between nutmeg and cloves, the reason why vanilla is the second most expensive spice by weight, and why ginger is so popular in Britain. He is immensely grateful to the early explorers who first brought back star anise, cinnamon, and strawberries, without which our cooking would be much duller. What would pasta be without tomatoes, or an apple pie without cinnamon? Just try to imagine a fruit salad without oranges, pineapple, or strawberries. To celebrate the culinary melting pot that French cuisine has become, Olivier Rœllinger has invented his signature dish, which goes by the rather grand name of Saint Pierre retour des Indes, or John Dory, the Voyage Back from the Indies, which incorporates the fourteen exotic spices commonly used in Saint Malo back in the eighteenth century.

Olivier Rœllinger's dream of uniting his two huge passions in life has proved a great success. Culinary traditions have always needed to incorporate new ingredients and flavors to avoid becoming dull and stale. In his restaurant in the small seaside town of Cancale, Rœllinger likes nothing better than to experiment with new combinations, testing out new ideas until he feels he knows every facet of every

dish. No combination of ingredients, however outlandish it might seem, is rejected out of hand. Sometimes the strangest marriages are the most harmonious. Every chef likes to change his tune once in a while. But he also acknowledges that, if a culinary tradition is cut off from its roots, like a plant, it will wither and die. Rœllinger's own cuisine is firmly rooted in centuries of fine Breton cooking. Many of his favorite ingredients come from the sea, bought fresh from the trawlers that are crewed by the men he grew up with. His cooking bears the stamp of the endless glowering skies, the salty earth, and the rushing tides of Brittany. Every Saturday he makes the round trip to the regional capital, Rennes, to buy the freshest ingredients from the market, where he knows the traders share his deep love and respect for the noble Breton traditions. He swears by quality, working in close collaboration with local producers of organic fruit and vegetables. Protecting the environment is second nature to a chef who believes that the finest ingredients are those that are grown and harvested in accordance with nature's laws. One reason why he loves seafood so much is that, as yet, it is relatively free from the pressures of multinational agro-businesses.

A chef's individual style depends very much on how in tune he is with the needs and demands of the day. The finest chefs of the past—Menon, Carême, Nignon, and, more recently, Michel Guérard—all instinctively understood that they had to work within a tradition, but married it with their own vision of its future development. Michel Guérard, for instance, was the first to realize that French cuisine was too reliant on rich sauces that were too heavy for this health-conscious age. He thus invented the concept of dietary cuisine in tune with his times.

Olivier Rœllinger's own contribution to this development has been to realize that people are keen to hark back to a less technological age, when food was as much about simplicity and well-being as about pleasure. He has created a cuisine that is bursting with health and kind to the environment. He is striving to create a new French cuisine that is cheeky, exciting, and surprising. His credo is that cooking should not be a way of reinforcing our differences, but of bringing us together.

Whether in cooking or in life, Olivier Rœllinger brings the spirit of adventure to everything he does.

Anne Testut

Pepper: The black pearl
latitude 9°58′ N, longitude 76°13′6″ E

India. Pepper is native to the Malabar Coast in India, where the locals have known it as *pilpali* for centuries.

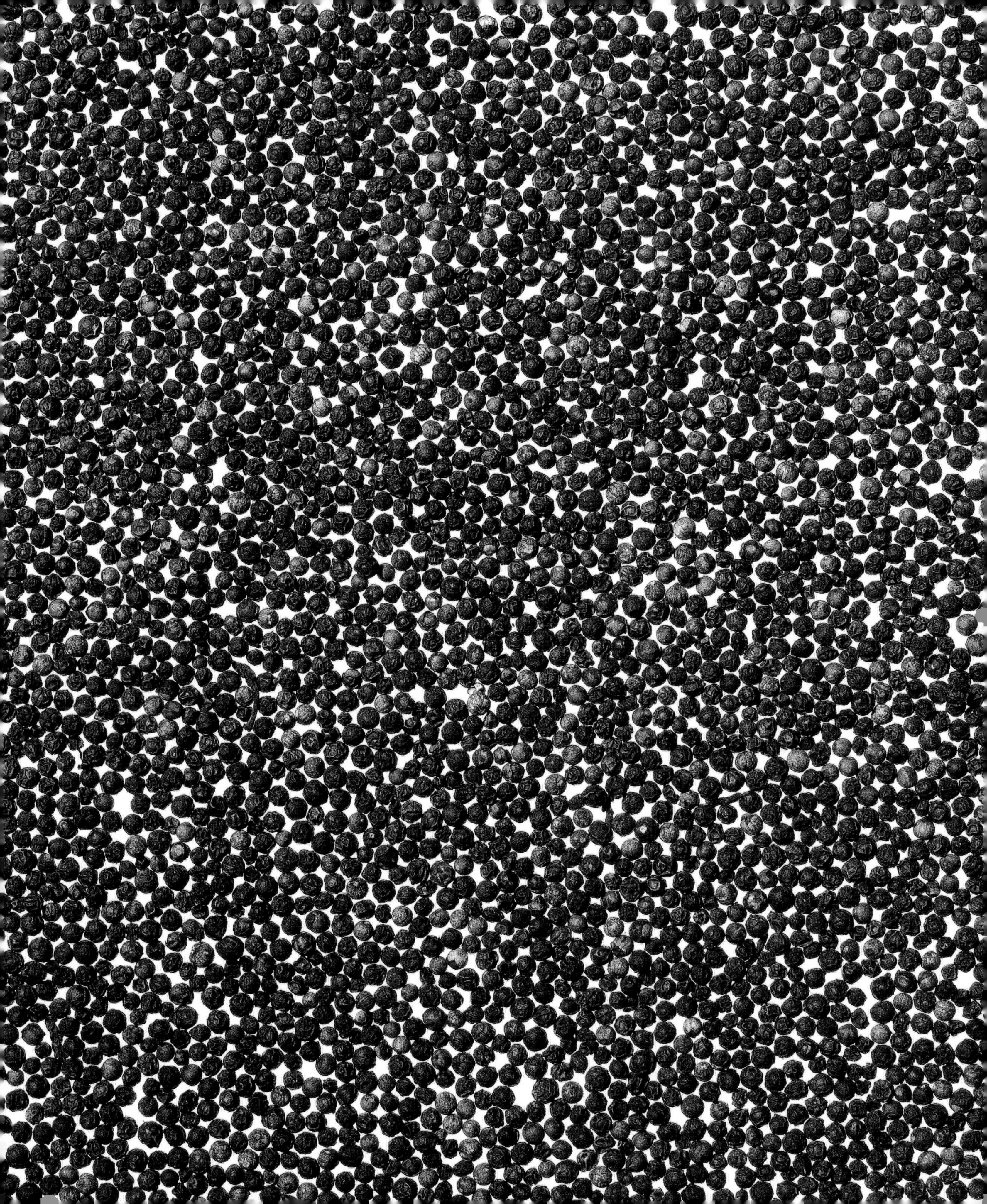

History

Pepper is native to the Malabar Coast in India, where the locals have known it as *pilpali* for centuries. News about the precious black berries gradually spread to the West. Pepper first became known in Persia before reaching Egypt and then ancient Greece. The Romans couldn't get enough of it. Pepper quickly became a sign of wealth, literally worth its weight in gold. Such was its value that a considerable trade in pepper sprang up between the West and the Orient via the Middle East. Indeed, one of the reasons that Alexander the Great led his armies as far as the shores of the River Indus was his wish to conquer the land where pepper grew so that he could control its supply. The same reasons led the great maritime nations of Europe to seek trade routes across the oceans a few centuries later.

The first modern European to discover pepper was said to have been the Portuguese explorer Vasco de Gama, who weighed anchor in Calicut—now Calcutta—in India on May 14, 1498. This date is significant: the discovery of America in 1492 meant there was now a new maritime trade route. This was to lay the foundations of the fortunes of the companies set up to profit from the precious spice. England, Portugal, Holland, and France all established East India companies. It is hardly an exaggeration to say that the search for a ready supply of pepper brought East and West together.

Natural history

Peppercorns are the berries of a tall climbing shrub that can grow to a height of six meters, or some eighteen feet, in the wild. *Piper nigrum* is a member of the *Piperaceae* family. The plant flourishes in warm, humid climates. The four types of pepper all come from the same plant, and how they are classified depends on the ripeness of the berries when they are picked.

- Green peppercorns are picked when the berries are still very unripe. They are then bottled in brine or freeze-dried.
- Black peppercorns are picked just as the berries begin to turn red, shortly before they attain perfect ripeness. They are then sun-dried, which naturally desiccates the berries.
- White peppercorns are picked when they are perfectly ripe. The berries are soaked in seawater and then rubbed to remove the red skin.
- Red peppercorns are picked when the fresh berries are perfectly ripe for immediate use.

Qualities

The delicate aroma of pepper harmonizes with a deep, complex flavor that is warm, rounded, long, strong, and intense. White pepper is not as strong as black, but its aroma is just as delicate. Black pepper has a less tame flavor. Pepper could be described as a catalyst for other flavors, bringing out their nuances and subtleties. While salt underlines the flavor of a dish, pepper is more like an exclamation mark. While a reasonable intake of salt is necessary for good health, pepper is purely a question of taste. It is now used to enhance flavor in dishes all over the world. Our cuisine would be insipid and dull without it.

Uses

Since the aroma of pepper is very volatile, the corns should be crushed or ground at the very last moment to preserve the flavor. While it has become second nature to use pepper in savory dishes, many people are unaware that a hint of freshly-ground pepper in desserts can add a surprising yet satisfying bite. The taste of pepper gives desserts a bit of a kick while rounding out the other ingredients. If you are the kind of diner who gives a couple of twists of the pepper mill to a bowl of soup or a roast before even tasting it, may I suggest you hold back next time? Pepper deserves to be appreciated in its own right. I particularly enjoy pepper on peri-winkles, oysters, pâté de foie gras, cep mushrooms, egg yolk, tuna, and, of course, strawberries. For my freshly-ground pepper, I always choose black pepper, which has a woodier, more aromatic note. I also prefer using black pepper for the pepper mills in my restaurant.

I do enjoy experimenting with mixing different peppers from different places to marry their subtly different tastes. The little round, wrinkled corns have become the symbol of the trade that forged links between peoples. And while pepper has conquered the world, it also has the virtue of letting the unique identity of each regional cuisine shine through.

The finest peppers

In terms of black pepper, my personal favorite is Malabar garbled grade 1 from the Peryar and Sultan Battery regions, although Lampong pepper from Sumatra in Indonesia is generally held to be the finest in the world. As for white pepper, I recommend Muntok from the island of Bangha to the southwest of Sumatra.

True pepper—*piper nigrum*—only has one true relative: long pepper or *piper longum*. It does have a number of "cousins," however, similar in taste but from entirely different families, including:

- Szechuan pepper, which has a lemony, aniseed flavor.
- Cubeb pepper, also known as Java or tailed pepper, which grows in the islands of Indonesia. It has a gentler flavor, and was much in favor in the Middle Ages until the Portuguese forbade traders from dealing in it so that they could boost their own trade in black pepper.
- *Piper methystium*, which grows on the islands of the Pacific, and which the Polynesians use to brew the alcoholic beverage known as kava-kava.
- Betel pepper from the Far East, which is mixed with ground limestone and areca nut to form a wad. This is then chewed like tobacco.
- Malagueta pepper, also known as grains of paradise or Guinea pepper, which deserves to be more widely known.
- Pink pepper, grown in great quantities in La Réunion, but which is in fact an aromatic berry native to America.

To determine the quality of the peppercorns, crush a few between two sheets of paper. The more oil they leave on the paper, the better they are.

My most treasured memory of pepper is the Cochin pepper futures exchange.

Health benefits

Pepper stimulates the body and acts as a tonic. It has an energizing effect on the digestive system in particular. It has antibacterial properties that can be used to preserve foodstuffs. As far as I am concerned, life would be duller without the spicy kick of pepper.

Setting the Course—As winter comes to an end, we head first for the Chemin des Douaniers, a path hugging the intricate outline of cliffs on which tiny sorrel leaves are already poking out of the ground. When we sample some, we're surprised by the metallic flavor afforded by the arid rock—it will lend a perfect touch of acidity to the oysters. Earthy slices of duck foie gras are topped with all the other ingredients, sharpened with a hint of hazelnut, and sustained by "black pearls"—the pepper.

Wild Cliff Sorrel, Oysters, Foie Gras,

Crew of 4

Rigging
Oyster knife
Small handheld blender
Mortar
4 plates

Cruising Time
2 hours

From the Ship's Hold
White Rully or Côtes-du-Jura

Provisions

Galley Pantry 1
24 no.1 flat oysters
7 oz. (200 g) high-quality terrine of duck foie gras
24 leaves cliff sorrel

Galley Pantry 2
Marinade for the Oysters
2 tbs sherry vinegar
3 tbs grape-seed oil
4 tbs hazelnut oil
4 tbs walnut oil

March 2, 2001. North wind, force 4 to 5. Blustery sky.

First Tack

Preheat oven to 400°F (200°C). Place hazelnuts (Galley Pantry 4) in shallow pan and toast lightly for 5 to 10 minutes until light blond in color. Check frequently to make sure the nuts do not become too dark. Cool.

Second Tack

Open oysters (Galley Pantry 1) and remove from shells, retaining root. Collect the oyster liquor, strain into a bowl, and add the shucked oysters. Refrigerate.

Third Tack

Prepare the oyster marinade (Galley Pantry 2). Place the sherry vinegar and grape-seed, hazelnut, and walnut oils in a bowl. Add salt and pepper to taste, whip until blended. Set aside. Crush the toasted hazelnuts in a mortar, set aside. Gently heat the Szechuan pepper in a small, ungreased saucepan. When the pepper reaches the fragrance point, remove from pan and crush in mortar. Add the largest hazelnut chunks and crush again. Add the rest of the crushed hazelnuts and the chopped chives (Galley Pantry 4).

Fourth Tack

Prepare the hazelnut emulsion (Galley Pantry 3). Select a bowl large enough to accommodate the handheld blender. Place in the bowl, in the following order: the white Chardonnay-wine vinegar, grape-seed and hazelnut oils. Blend. Add the reserved oyster liquor and the egg white. Blend again. Cut the duck foie gras (Galley Pantry 1) into 24 slices (depending on the shape of the terrine—12 slices cut in 2, for example). Arrange the rectangles of foie gras on serving plates.

Landfall

Strain the oysters, place in a single layer on a clean dishtowel, sponge dry. Arrange leaves of sorrel (Galley Pantry 1) on one side of each foie gras rectangle. Work quickly for the following steps: place all the oysters in a bowl with the marinade, marinate for 2 minutes. Meanwhile, dribble lines of the emulsion on either side of the rows of foie gras and sorrel. Arrange the oysters on top of the foie-gras slices, sprinkle with the pulverized hazelnuts. Serve.

and Hazelnut Oil

Galley Pantry 3
Hazelnut Emulsion

1 egg white
2 tbs white Chardonnay-wine vinegar
3 tbs grape-seed oil
10 tbs hazelnut oil
2 tbs oyster liquor

Galley Pantry 4
Crushed Hazelnuts and Szechuan Pepper

25 dried hazelnuts, skinned
1 tsp Szechuan pepper
20 chives

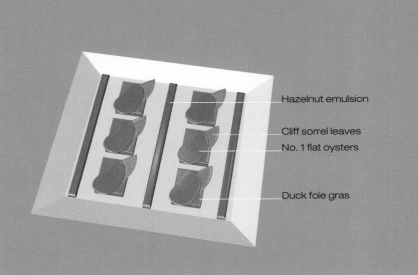

Hazelnut emulsion

Cliff sorrel leaves
No. 1 flat oysters

Duck foie gras

Setting the Course—Abalone is a mystery, even to the natives of Saint-Malo. This shellfish is visible only at very low tide. Otherwise it must be groped for blindly, underwater. It takes a lot of experience to recognize the abalone lurking under a rock, and it takes strength and skill to pry it loose. The reward is well worth the effort, however. The interior of the gleaming mother-of-pearl shell exudes a heady and powerful odor of the sea and all its riches. A smell of the depths, the zestful scent of stones uncovered by the receding tide. Its characteristic flavor and texture makes abalone the greatest prize in the shore fisherman's basket, the finest catch in the sea.

Cancale Abalone

Crew of 4

Rigging
Small, stiff brush
Small handheld blender
Pair of kitchen shears
Strainer
2 nonstick frying pans
4 plates

Cruising Time
3 days

From the Ship's Hold
Savennières or dry Riesling grand cru

Provisions

Galley Pantry 1
12 abalone
1 shallot
1 clove garlic
4 tbs sherry vinegar
2 tbs (25 g) + 1 ½ tbs (20 g) salted butter

Galley Pantry 2
Sauce
Abalone barbels
1 tbs grape-seed oil
1 tsp (15 g) butter
1 clove garlic
2 shallots
2 sprigs flat parsley
2 tbs sherry vinegar
5 tbs white Port wine
1 tbs mixed seaweed (nori, wakamé, sea lettuce, kombu)
8 tbs chicken bouillon

September 1984. East wind, force 4 to 5. Rough sea.

First Tack

Purchase the live abalone 3 days beforehand (Galley Pantry 1). Wrap the shellfish in a damp cloth and refrigerate. All the other Tacks can be carried out during the 3 hours before serving the meal.

Second Tack

Prepare the abalone (Galley Pantry 1). Use a knife to remove from shells. Select 8 of the best-looking shells, brush, scald, and drain. Remove intestines from shells. Use kitchen shears to cut off the barbels, brush and rinse the abalone under running water. Wrap each abalone separately in a clean cloth and knead to tenderize the flesh. Season with salt and freshly-ground black pepper.

Third Tack

The sauce (Galley Pantry 2): Wash and drain the reserved barbels, sauté in 1 tbs grape-seed oil until golden. Add the butter, garlic, chopped shallots, and chopped sprigs of parsley. Sauté this mixture for 2 to 3 minutes and deglaze pan with the sherry vinegar. Add the white Port wine and bring to boil. Add the seaweed and chicken bouillon. Simmer 30 minutes and strain, pressing firmly to extract all the liquid. Set aside. The parsley oil (Galley Pantry 3). Stem the parsley, scald the leaves for 2 minutes in a large pot of boiling salted water, refresh in ice water. This operation will stabilize the chlorophyll. Drain the scalded parsley leaves, pressing firmly to extract all the liquid. Add the grape-seed oil and blend. Strain this mixture and set aside.

Fourth Tack

Final preparation. Peel and chop the shallot; peel the garlic clove (Galley Pantry 1). Prepare the garnish (Galley Pantry 4). One hour before serving, cook the whole, unpeeled potatoes. Wash the mushrooms, drain, set aside. When the potatoes are cooked, peel and add 2 tbs (25 g) butter. Mash with a fork and set aside in a warm place.

Landfall

Heat the sunflower oil in a small saucepan and briefly fry the 12 large leaves of flat parsley (Galley Pantry 4). Drain on absorbent paper and set aside. Preheat 1 frying pan for the mushrooms and another for the abalone. Sauté the mushrooms quickly in 2 tbs (25 g) butter, season with salt and pepper. Sauté the abalone in 2 tbs (25 g) butter (Galley Pantry 1), turning until golden on both sides. Add the shallot and garlic (Galley Pantry 1). Continue to cook gently until done. Set aside the abalone. Deglaze the pans with 4 tbs sherry vinegar. Reduce by one-half. Add the abalone liquor. Reduce until slightly syrupy. Lastly, add the remaining 1 ½ tbs (20 g) butter. Arrange the abalone diagonally on 4 large heated serving plates. Fill the cleaned shells with the mashed potato, top with the mushrooms and fried parsley leaves. Place the filled shells on the outer edge of the plates. Cover each abalone with sauce. Place 1 teaspoon of the parsley oil opposite each shell. Serve.

Galley Pantry 3
Parsley Oil
½ bunch flat parsley
8 tbs grape-seed oil

Galley Pantry 4
Garnish
4 new potatoes
2 tbs (25 g) salted butter + 2 tbs (25 g) salted butter
¾ lb. (300 g) wild mushrooms (chanterelle, craterellus, etc.)
12 large leaves flat parsley
½ cup (10 cl) sunflower oil

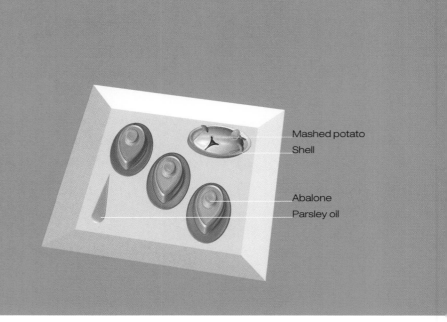

Mashed potato
Shell

Abalone
Parsley oil

Setting the Course—Shelled shrimp with bread and butter is a treat to be shared at the seashore in reverent silence. Here is perfection of a kind, a pleasure it would be hard to surpass. And yet during one summer's heat wave I felt the need for something different at aperitif time, and created this subtle combination of cool aspic and sensual saffron, accented with an unexpected hint of long pepper.

Shrimp in Aspic with Christe-Marine

Crew of 4

Rigging
Mason jar
Small handheld blender
Small strainer
Coffee mill
4 soup plates
4 small bowls

Cruising Time
24 hours

From the Ship's Hold
Cassis or Entre-Deux-Mers

Provisions

Galley Pantry 1
Shrimp Aspic
¾ lb. (300 g) + ¼ lb. (100 g) shrimps
1 tbs galingale (or approx. 1 kernel)
3 cumbava leaves (from a small lemon tree native
    to Thailand)
½ stick citronella
3 cups (¾ liter) chicken bouillon
3 sheets seaweed gelatine (agar-agar)

Galley Pantry 2
Saffron Emulsion
4 tbs water
½ teaspoon saffron pistils
⅔ cup (15 cl) grape-seed oil
1 tbs sherry vinegar
1 egg white
Pinch of salt
Pepper

July 9, 2001. Calm sea, good visibility.

First Tack

The sweet-sour zucchini (Galley Pantry 3): Wash the zucchini thoroughly, cut in quarters lengthwise, remove seeds, chop, and transfer to Mason jar. Place the water, sugar, salt, 5 tbs rice vinegar, peppercorns, juniper berries, coriander seeds, clove, and christe-marine (Galley Pantry 4) in a pot. Bring to a boil and pour into the Mason jar. Add the remaining 1 tbs rice vinegar and close the jar. Refrigerate overnight. Prepare the finishing touches (Galley Pantry 4). Grind the long pepper in a coffee mill, add the fleur de sel, stir and set aside.

Second Tack

The shrimp aspic (Galley Pantry 1): Peel the shrimps, reserve heads and shells. Refrigerate the peeled shrimps. Peel and chop the galingale. Chop the 3 leaves of cumbava and the citronella (Galley Pantry 1). Place the chicken bouillon, the shrimps, the reserved shrimp heads and shells, and the spices in a pot. Bring to a boil. Reduce the heat and simmer for 1 hour. Strain. Whip in the gelatine. Place in a glass bowl and refrigerate.

Third Tack

Blanch the christe-marine (Galley Pantry 4) and refresh in cold water. Reserve the 4 most shapely trident stems and chop the rest. Next prepare the plates of aspic. The aspic in the pot will have separated. Remove the clear upper portion, heat it gently, and discard the rest. When the aspic is liquid, pour it into 4 soup plates and sprinkle with the chopped christe-marine. Refrigerate until set. The saffron emulsion (Galley Pantry 2): Bring 4 tbs water to boiling point, add the saffron, remove from heat, cover, and infuse for 15 minutes. In a bowl, combine the grape-seed oil, sherry vinegar, salt, pepper, and egg white. Whip with small handheld blender until smooth. Add the entire contents of the pot and whip again. If the mixture is too thick, add a little water.

Landfall

Drain the zucchini. Arrange alternating rows of zucchini and shrimp on top of the aspic. Pour a little of the saffron emulsion between the rows. Garnish with sprigs of christe-marine and sprinkle with a little fleur de sel and pepper. Fill small bowls with the remaining emulsion. Serve.

_ong Pepper, and a Hint of Saffron

Galley Pantry 3
Sweet-Sour Zucchini
1 medium zucchini
5 tbs + 1 tbs rice vinegar
1 cup (25 cl) water
1 tbs sugar
1 tsp salt
5 black peppercorns
5 white peppercorns
10 coriander seeds
3 juniper berries
1 clove
2 sprigs christe-marine

Galley Pantry 4
Finishing
1 tbs long pepper
1 tsp fleur de sel
A few sprigs christe-marine

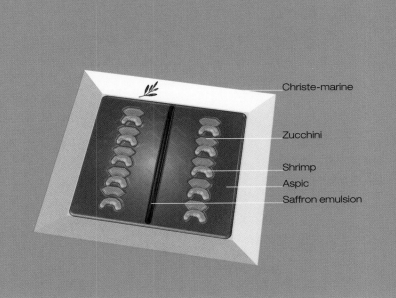

Christe-marine

Zucchini

Shrimp
Aspic
Saffron emulsion

Setting the Course—Fish shouldn't be killed a second time by brutal cooking methods! At Kerala in south-west India, on the Malabar coast, I found a terracotta dish similar to the tajine of North Africa, but with a rounded base that makes the cooking even gentler. The delicate, difficult-to-cook flesh of sea bass becomes smooth and silky in this mixture of bouillon and elderflower oil with its aroma of late wine harvests.

Sea Bass Cooked Gently in Fragrant

Crew of Four

Rigging
Strainer
Japanese mandolin
2 Mason jars
Pair of kitchen shears
Small handheld blender
Terracotta dish or traditional tajine measuring
   8 x 11 in. (20 x 30 cm)
4 soup plates

Cruising Time
24 hours

From the Ship's Hold
Dry Riesling grand cru

Provisions

Galley Pantry 1
The fish
1 whole sea bass weighing 3–4 lb. (1.5 to 2 kg)

Galley Pantry 2
Elderflower Oil
This oil is available ready-mixed at Les Maisons de Bricourt.
½ cup (12 cl) grape-seed oil
5 elderflower blooms

June 7, 2001. Wind from the west, force 3 to 4. Large, high-altitude cumulus clouds.

First Tack

The elderflower oil (Galley Pantry 2): Pick the elderflower blooms on a clear day, when the sun is at its highest. Cut off the white flowers. Place the blooms and grape-seed oil in a Mason jar. Close tightly and sterilize in a boiling-water bath for 10 minutes, counting from second boil. Set aside to cool and allow to steep overnight. The remaining preparations can be done a few hours before serving.

Second Tack

Prepare the garnish (Galley Pantry 4). Shell the broad beans, cook for 5 minutes in boiling salted water. Refresh without removing the skins. Set aside. Dice the scraped carrots, rind of 3 lemons, and zucchini peel. Toss into boiling salted water and cook for 1 minute after second boil. Drain and refresh under cold water to preserve color. Set aside.

Third Tack

Prepare the fish (Galley Pantry 1). Scale and rinse the fish, cut away the fillets, remove the bones. Cut the fillets into 8 equal portions. Place the portions of fish in a terracotta dish and refrigerate. Moules marinière (Galley Pantry 3): First, sauté the chopped shallot in the sunflower oil. Add the parsley sprigs, mussels, and white wine. Cover and bring to boil. Continue to cook, covered, for 8 minutes. Drain, reserving the cooking liquid. The mussels can be saved to use in another dish.

Fourth Tack

Sauce and final cooking. In a large Mason jar, combine the basil oil, lemon juice (Galley Pantry 3), strained elderflower oil, and liquid from the mussels. Sprinkle with pepper. Close jar tightly and shake vigorously. Pour this mixture over the fish fillets until they are barely covered. Seal the dish with aluminum foil.

Landfall

Preheat oven to 300°F (150°C). Bake the covered fish for 15 minutes. Check frequently for doneness. When cooked, transfer fish from oven and gently remove the skin. Reheat the broad beans rapidly in a pan with a little water and a knob of butter. Reheat the diced vegetables. Strain the cooking liquid from the fish into a pan and keep hot. Divide the portions of sea bass equally between four heated soup plates, garnish with a spoonful of the diced vegetables, and surround with the broad beans. Blend the hot sauce until it forms an emulsion and pour over the fish. Sprinkle with a little freshly-ground Malabar pepper and serve.

Oils

Galley Pantry 3
Moules Marinière
2 lb. (500 g) mussels
1 large shallot
1 tbs sunflower oil
2 sprigs parsley
1 cup (25 cl) white wine
5 tbs basil oil
6 tbs lemon juice

Galley Pantry 4
Garnish
3 lb. (1.5 kg) broad beans
2 large zucchini
2 small baby carrots
3 lemons
1 knob butter

Finishing
Malabar pepper

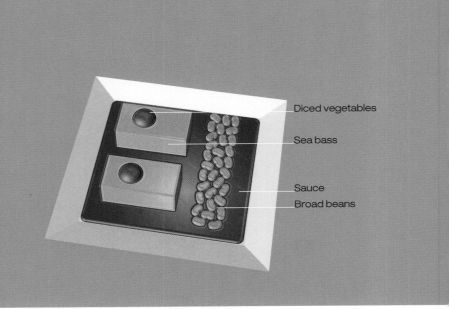

Diced vegetables

Sea bass

Sauce

Broad beans

Setting the Course—Apricots can be delicious, but today they're often tasteless. Knowing how to select them makes all the difference. I'm often put off by their skin texture and bitter taste. Apricot pulp acquires a hint of almond from the pit, and a sensual flavor enhanced by heat. To contrast with the fruit's acidity, and to lend an Oriental note, I add small cubes provocatively scented with rose water—like miniature pieces of Turkish delight, but less sugary. These flavor and texture contrasts are further accentuated by the coconut-milk pepper crisps.

Warm Apricot Pulp with Rose-Water

Crew of Four

Rigging
Nonstick baking sheet
Purée strainer
Square of muslin measuring 4 in. x 4 in. (10 x 10 cm)
Candy thermometer
Wax paper
Square tin measuring 4 in. x 4 in. (9 x 9 cm)
4 Chinese bowls

Cruising Time
24 hours

From the Ship's Hold
Muscat de Frontignan or late-harvested Gewürztraminer

Provisions

Galley Pantry 1
Rose-Water Paste
⅔ cup (175 g) sugar
½ cup (10 cl) water
½ tsp (5 g) agar-agar, or seaweed gelatin dissolved in
   ¼ cup (5 cl) water
4 drops rose water (or more, depending on strength)
1 tbs confectioner's sugar
1 tbs cornstarch

Galley Pantry 2
Apricot Pulp
1 ½ lb. (600 g) very ripe apricots
½ Bourbon vanilla pod
½ cup (120 g) water
½ cup (120 g) sugar

July 22, 2004. Calm seas, heat mist, late-evening tropical breeze.

First Tack

The day before serving, prepare the tiny squares of rose-water paste (Galley Pantry 1). Place the sugar and ½ cup (10 cl) water in a small pan, bring to the boil and cook until the syrup stage, or 239°F (115°C) on a candy thermometer. Remove pan from heat and add the agar dissolved in ¼ cup (5 cl) water. Stir until blended. Return pan to heat and cook to a temperature of 225°F (107°C). Remove pan from heat and place in cold water in order to halt the cooking. Add the rose water, and stir. Line a 3–4 in. square (9 cm square) pan with wax paper and pour in the cooled syrup. Refrigerate for 24 hours.

Second Tack

Apricot pulp (Galley Pantry 2): Pit the apricots. Crush the pits and wrap in muslin. Make a syrup with the sugar, water, and vanilla. Bring to a boil, add the apricots and packet of apricot pits. Simmer for approximately 15 minutes. Remove the packet of apricot pits and discard. Blend the apricot pulp (using a handheld blender) until smooth. Strain this mixture through a purée strainer.

Third Tack

Pepper crisps (Galley Pantry 3): Stir the sifted flour, sugar, two peppers, green walnuts, and melted butter into the coconut milk. Set aside for 30 minutes. Using a teaspoon, place small strips of this pepper dough on a nonstick baking sheet. Bake for 5 minutes at the highest setting for your oven and remove immediately from baking sheet. Cool on rack and store in airtight tin.

Fourth Tack

Finishing the rose-water paste. Sift together the confectioner's sugar and cornstarch (Galley Pantry 1). Loosen the rose-water paste from pan, reverse pan over the sugar mixture, and shake out the paste. Peel off the wax paper and cut the paste into small squares. Dredge in the cornstarch mixture and store in an airtight tin.

Landfall

Serve the apricot pulp hot or cold, as desired. If too thick, add a little water. Pour the apricot pulp into the Chinese bowls, arrange the small rose-water squares on top, and garnish with a few pepper crisps.

Garnish, Pepper Crisps

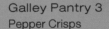

Galley Pantry 3
Pepper Crisps
2 tbs (25 g) flour
4 tbs (60 g) sugar
1 tsp cubeb pepper
1 tsp Szechuan pepper
1 tsp green walnuts
2 tbs (35 g) melted butter
4 tbs (50 g) coconut milk

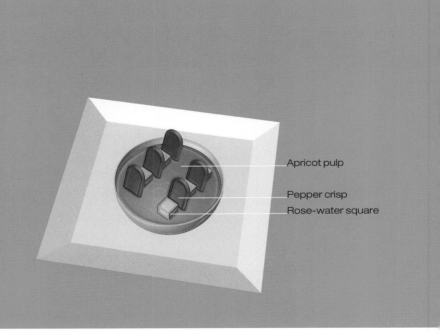

Apricot pulp

Pepper crisp
Rose-water square

Nutmeg: The noble seed
latitude 10°22′ S, longitude 127°40′ E

The Moluccas. The Chinese, Indians, and Europeans all discovered nutmeg at the same time. It quickly became one of their favorite spices.

History

The Chinese, Indians, and Europeans all discovered nutmeg at the same time. It quickly became one of their favorite spices. It was discovered by the Portuguese when they arrived in the archipelago of the Moluccas in 1512. After 1602, the Dutch had complete control of the market. They carefully guarded the island of Banda, and did not allow the spice to be grown anywhere else, to the point of uprooting plants on other islands. This meant that prices remained extremely high. The Dutch were pitiless with anyone caught stealing plants or nutmeg seeds. They even went so far as to soak the nutmeg in a water and limestone mix to prevent the seeds from germinating. To this day, many people believe that nutmeg is supposed to be whitish in color, when this was simply a side effect of the soaking process.

Eventually, two Frenchmen, Mahé de la Bourdonnais and Pierre Poivre, managed to get past the Dutch defenses and steal nutmeg and clove seedlings. Pierre Poivre was later appointed to oversee plantations in the French colonies of Réunion and Mauritius. He lost no time in transplanting his precious seedlings there, destroying the Dutch monopoly. Today, Europe is still the biggest market for nutmeg.

Natural history

Nutmeg is the seed of the tree *Myristica fragrans*. The nutmeg tree actually produces two spices—nutmeg and mace. The tree produces a pretty yellow fruit the size of an apricot which, when ripe, splits open to reveal a large, bright-red seed. The red fibrous covering—which produces mace—envelops the shell. When this covering is cracked, it reveals the nutmeg inside.

Qualities

Nutmeg has a rich, warm, slightly sweet taste. It is a rounded, sensuous spice. Mace is subtler in flavor, and slightly bitter.

Uses

Nutmeg is perfect for flavoring all sorts of dishes calling for milk, cream, and eggs. It also goes surprisingly well with potatoes and cauliflower. I like to use a small pinch of nutmeg to flavor the sauces I serve with seafood, such as a nage sauce, or lemon butter. It can also be used to accompany honey, pears, cherries, lemon, and any dish involving vanilla. It is one of my favorites, as it always evokes seafaring adventurers for me.

Nutmeg should always be freshly grated, as it loses its flavor very quickly when it is ready-ground.

The finest nutmeg

Funnily enough, nutmeg is hardly grown in its native Moluccas anymore. The best nutmeg now comes from the delightful island of Grenada in the southern Caribbean. The scent of nutmeg wafts over the island, perfuming the air. The discarded shells are used instead of gravel on smaller roads and paths.

Good nutmeg will have a regular brown color and will be relatively heavy, with a high density.

Health benefits

In the eighteenth century, nutmeg was used to cure a variety of ailments. Nutmeg butter is said to be very good for rheumatism.

Setting the Course—I've always wanted to combine the contrasting flavors of oyster and asparagus. This time I decided to improve on the idea with a suave, tart touch of nutmeg. When I look back on it today, this dish seems completely obvious—a simple, perfect union. The linseeds, apart from their health-giving properties, are delicious. Puffing them adds a "grilled" note.

Fresh Oysters and Asparagus, Puffed

Crew of Four

Rigging
Mason jar
Hammer
Strainer
Oyster knife
Small handheld blender
4 soup plates

Cruising Time
24 hours

From the Ship's Hold
Muscat d'Alsace

Provisions

Galley Pantry 1
24 no. 2 oysters
12 large stalks green asparagus

Galley Pantry 2
Nutmeg Sauce
1 poached egg
4 tbs oyster liquor
4 tbs Chardonnay-wine vinegar
8 tbs grape-seed oil
1 nutmeg
Dash of turmeric
Dash of cayenne pepper

May 3, 2003. Gale warning, force 6 to 7.

First Tack

Prepare the turmeric oil (Galley Pantry 3) at least one day in advance. Pour the grape-seed oil into a Mason jar and add the turmeric. Sterilize in a boiling-water bath for 10 minutes. Set aside.

Second Tack

A few hours at most before serving, wash and peel the asparagus (Galley Pantry 1). Open the oysters and shuck them (Galley Pantry 1), recovering as much of the oyster liquor as possible. Strain the liquor and place in a small pan with the oysters. Set aside. Puff the linseeds (Galley Pantry 4) by plunging them into a small pot of boiling sunflower oil. Cover the pot while the linseeds are cooking. When done, drain in a strainer and set aside.

Third Tack

The nutmeg sauce (Galley Pantry 2): Place the poached egg, oyster liquor, wine vinegar, and grape-seed oil in a large bowl. Mix together thoroughly. Crush the nutmeg with the hammer and add to the mixture in the bowl with the turmeric and Cayenne pepper.

Landfall

Prepare a double boiler for the nutmeg sauce. Cook the asparagus in boiling salted water. Trim the tough lower portion of the stems and set aside the spears. Place the nutmeg sauce in the top of the double boiler and heat, stirring constantly. When the sauce has thickened, remove from heat and strain immediately into a clean pot. Heat the oysters to lukewarm and arrange in large heated soup plates. Garnish with 3 asparagus tips and the chopped stems on one side, 6 oysters on the other. Pour the nutmeg sauce over the base of the asparagus spears. Garnish each oyster with puffed linseeds. Pour a few drops of the turmeric oil around the edge. Serve.

Linseeds, Turmeric

Galley Pantry 3
Turmeric Oil
½ cup (12 cl) grape-seed oil
1 tsp turmeric

Galley Pantry 4
Finishing
2 tbs linseeds
4 tbs sunflower oil

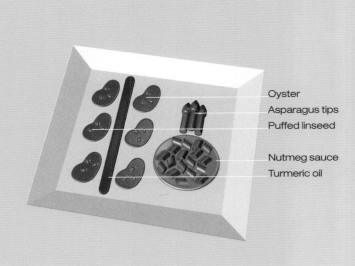

Oyster
Asparagus tips
Puffed linseed

Nutmeg sauce
Turmeric oil

Setting the Course—The subtle, nutty flavor of un-aged vinegar sustains the nutmeg—a marvelous accompaniment for a fish that is all too often mediocre due to a system of fish-farming for which we pay the highest price of all: loss of genuine flavor. But when the salmon is wild, and we take the trouble to cook it gently, it recovers all of its subtlety on the palate. This particular dish draws unexpected power from the malt, the Isle of Islay, and the fresh crispness of the apple.

Wild Salmon with Raw Apple, Nutmeg

Crew of Four

Rigging
Small handheld blender
Mortar for grinding spices
Coffee mill
Strainer
Japanese mandolin
4 soup plates

Cruising Time
24 hours

From the Ship's Hold
White Pessac-Léognan or white Anjou

Provisions

Galley Pantry 1
8 fillets of scaled, wild, unskinned salmon weighing 2–3 oz.
 (70 g) each

Galley Pantry 2
Nutmeg Powder
⅓ of a whole nutmeg
½ tsp coriander seeds
1 tsp fleur de sel
1 tsp pulverized almonds

June 21, 2004. Relatively calm sea, wind from the northwest, force 2 to 3.

First Tack

The night before, prepare the sauce (Galley Pantry 3). Place all ingredients in a pan. Heat until warm and pour into an airtight jar. Close jar and set aside until the next day.

Second Tack

One hour before serving, prepare the nutmeg powder (Galley Pantry 2). Crush the nutmeg in a mortar. Place the crushed nutmeg and coriander seeds in a coffee mill, grind, and transfer to a clean dish. Add the pulverized almonds and fleur de sel. Mix thoroughly and set aside.

Third Tack

Garnishes (Galley Pantry 4): Cut the pickles into matchsticks. Split the almonds in two and chop lengthwise. Mix together and set aside

Fourth Tack

Strain the sauce into a pot. Place the salmon fillets in a baking pan, skin side down, and sprinkle with the nutmeg powder.

Landfall

Preheat oven to 212°F (100°C). Place a shallow pan of water in the bottom of the oven to humidify it. Bake the salmon fillets for 15 minutes. Chop the coriander and mint leaves (Galley Pantry 4). Use the Japanese mandolin to slice the ½ apple, then cut each slice into shoestrings. Mix together the pickles, almonds, coriander, mint, and apple. Heat the sauce, without boiling, and blend. Remove skin from salmon fillets and place 2 fillets in each of the 4 soup plates. Spread the garnish on half of each fillet. Cover with sauce and serve.

and Mace

Galley Pantry 3
Sauce
3 tbs cider vinegar
1 tsp coriander seeds
3 tbs nuoc-mâm
1 tbs Islay Single Malt
5 tbs quality olive oil
6 tbs grape-seed oil
5 tbs water
½ tsp mace

Galley Pantry 4
Garnishes
5 small sour pickles
10 shelled, peeled almonds
10 coriander leaves
5 mint leaves
½ Granny Smith apple

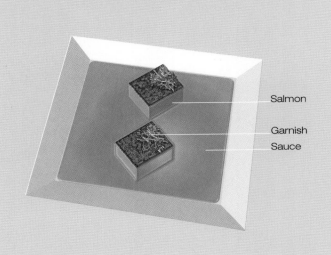

Salmon

Garnish
Sauce

Setting the Course—The character of this dish draws on the taste of stony cliffs, shellfish, wild herbs, and the sea. I thought of the combination of ingredients one winter's afternoon while enjoying a zestful bottle of wine beside the sea, as waves rolled in on the great currents from the south and broke on the shore. There they acquired a hint of buckwheat, the "white" grain that saved generations of Bretons from famine. This particular blend, with its evocation of a rockbound coast, might be compared to a great Islay Single Malt. Heather, pine, privet, seaweed, sea spray, iodine, and sulfur form the base, heightened with spices from faraway climes. A dish with the flavor of sea winds.

Warm Flat Oysters, Herb Compote,

40

Crew of Four

Rigging
Mason jar
Small handheld blender
Strainer
4 plates

Cruising Time
3 hours

From the Ship's Hold
Chinon Blanc

Provisions

Galley Pantry 1
24 medium flat oysters

Galley Pantry 2
Herb Compote
1 large onion
1 clove garlic
1 knob butter
8 leaves poultry curry (or 16 leaves fresh coriander)
1 tbs cumin seeds
1 nutmeg, crushed
1 cup (25 cl) chicken bouillon
1 bottle Chateldon (sparkling mineral water)
1 bunch watercress
½ lb. (200 g) fresh spinach

March 15, 2004. Chill wind from northwest, force 3 to 4. Rough seas.

First Tack

A few hours before serving, prepare the herb compote (Galley Pantry 2). Chop the onion, crush the peeled garlic clove. Sauté these ingredients in a knob of butter without allowing them to color. Add the chopped poultry curry, cumin, and crushed nutmeg. Add the chicken bouillon. Simmer this compote until thick. Cool. Stem and wash the watercress and spinach. Bring the Chateldon water to a boil, add the spinach and watercress, scald, and refresh directly in ice. Reserve the cooking liquid. Drain the spinach and watercress. Set aside.

Second Tack

Prepare the buckwheat garnish (Galley Pantry 3). For the boiled buckwheat: wash the peeled buckwheat, drain well. Sauté in 2 tbs olive oil. Add 2 cups water, cover, and simmer for 20 minutes. The buckwheat should absorb all the water. Season when done. Place the cooked buckwheat in a strainer and rinse well in order to wash out all crushed grains. Chop the chives and set aside. For the fried buckwheat: heat 4 tbs grape-seed oil and fry 2 tbs (unwashed) buckwheat until light brown. Drain. Season with salt and place in an airtight container.

Third Tack

Shuck the 24 oysters (Galley Pantry 1), reserving as much of the liquor as possible. Strain the oyster liquor into a pan and add the shucked oysters. Finishing the herb compote (Galley Pantry 2): Place the scalded spinach and watercress in a large bowl, along with the compote prepared at the beginning of the recipe. Blend and add ¼ of the cooking liquid (the Chateldon water). Blend again and strain. Press the contents of the strainer with the back of a spoon to obtain a maximum of pulp. Set the herb compote aside in a pot.

Landfall

Serve in large warmed plates. Reheat the boiled buckwheat and the fried buckwheat quickly in a pot with a knob of butter. Add the chives. Warm the oysters in their liquor to a maximum temperature of 104°F (40°C). Heat the herb compote without boiling. Arrange three alternating rows of oysters and buckwheat on each plate and pour the herb compote between the rows. Serve.

and Buckwheat

Galley Pantry 3
Buckwheat Garnish
Boiled buckwheat:
1 cup skinned buckwheat
2 cups water
2 tbs olive oil
A few chives

Fried Buckwheat:
2 tbs skinned buckwheat
4 tbs grape-seed oil

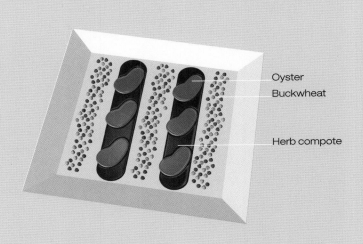

Oyster
Buckwheat

Herb compote

Cloves: The Christmas bud
latitude 4°25′ S, longitude 125°41′ E

The Moluccas. Cloves were considered highly mysterious for centuries because of their shape—like tiny tacks—and their powerful flavor, not to mention their place of origin, the far-distant Moluccas.

48–49
Light Camembert Cream, Asparagus, Cloves

50–51
Grog with Brittany Cider and Marie-
Galante Rum

History

Cloves were considered highly mysterious for centuries because of their shape—like tiny tacks—and their powerful flavor, not to mention their place of origin, the far-distant Moluccas. For centuries they were so rare that they exchanged hands for astronomical sums, far higher even than the staggering prices paid for nutmeg or saffron. Dealing in cloves was even held to be a sign of distinction, which is why in the Middle Ages the French guild of "sovereign pepper merchants," the precursors of apothecaries and grocers, emblazoned their coat of arms with peppercorns and cloves.

The origins of the highly sought-after buds remained a mystery until the end of the Middle Ages. Some people even believed that they grew in the earthly ruins of the Garden of Eden at the ends of the earth, where the sun rises.

In reality the precious spice was brought from the Moluccas to Venice by Chinese and Arab merchants, who sailed along the coasts of India and Africa before bringing their valuable cargo overland by camel as far as Alexandria, where it was loaded onto ships bound for Venice. Once the various taxes, customs duties, and other costs had been added to the price, the cloves were sold a few at a time to the royal courts and noble households of Europe.

The first Europeans to reach the Moluccas—islands rich in cloves and nutmeg trees—were the Portuguese, thanks to Vasco da Gama's daring in sailing around the horn of Africa to reach the Indies. At the same time, in 1512, the city of Malacca, then under Arab control, fell into the hands of Afonso de Albuquerque. These two events meant that the Portuguese had absolute control over the supply of cloves for the best part of a century. Lisbon became the principal trading center for cloves, breaking the monopoly of the Arabs and Venetians.

However, the Dutch were eager to break into the highly lucrative market, and soon wrested the monopoly from the Portuguese. Cloves became more widely available as the price fell by more than half. In those days, the buds were dried in barrels or strung on string like a rosary. But the Dutch were well aware that it was in their interest to keep prices high, as with nutmeg. To maintain a high price, they set up one of the earliest international financial speculations. They uprooted all the clove plantations in the Moluccas, with the exception of those on the island of Amboine. Once they had the harvest under control, they would build up the stocks over several seasons. As the regular supply dried up, the prices shot sky-high. The British and later the French were keen to put an end to this policy of financial speculation and get their own hands on supplies of nutmeg and cloves.

Once more, it was the Frenchmen Mahé de la Bourdonnais and Pierre Poivre who managed to steal seedlings from under the noses of the Dutch, and plant them in French colonies with similar climates. The very first seedlings were planted in the famous Pamplemousses gardens in Mauritius. The Dutch monopoly was broken. Over the years, cloves began to be grown in Madagascar, the Caribbean, and in Guyana.

Natural history
Cloves are the flower bud of the beautiful tropical tree *Eugenia caryophyllata*, which can reach heights of some thirty feet (ten meters). The cloves are picked by hand and dried in the sun, when they quickly take on their characteristic brown color.

Qualities
The unique aromatic flavor of cloves is due to a highly scented oil rich in eugenol, which gives it its warm, sensual aroma.

Uses
Cloves can be used whole or ground in a variety of ways. For centuries, people have stuck cloves into lemons or oranges as a way of perfuming a room. It is hardly original, but I love cloves with onion. In fact, they go well with all members of the onion and garlic family. They are also an indispensable ingredient in court bouillon and fish stock. They bring an elegant touch to curries when married with pepper, nutmeg, cinnamon, and ginger. The first impression of the taste of cloves is unique. I use ground cloves in nearly all my spice mixes for the almost numbing quality it has on the tongue. Take care when using cloves, because their powerful flavor can easily overpower more delicate ingredients. Personally, I find that they underline the smooth, sweet notes of other ingredients to perfection.

The finest cloves
The finest cloves grow on islands. The best of all come from Grenada in the Caribbean, the island of Pemba near Zanzibar, and Saint Mary's Island, northeast of Madagascar.

Health benefits
Cloves have been used in Chinese, Indian, and European cuisine for centuries because of their antibacterial and antifungal properties. They are also used to soothe toothache. In fact, eugenol is now extracted from cloves for use in dentistry. Cloves are also a powerful antioxidant.

Setting the Course—Here's a wonderful treat for spring. At the end of winter, every new bud and tiny sprout expresses extraordinary organic vitality, and I've created a delectable dish to reflect this exciting cycle of rebirth. Asparagus, a regal vegetable whose reign is all too brief, is at its peak in spring. My wonderful idea is to submerge it in a creamy sauce of deeply satisfying Camembert. Here is my overture to spring, the season when Mother Nature is at her very best.

Light Camembert Cream, Asparagus

48

Crew of Four	Provisions
Rigging	**Galley Pantry 1**
Mason jar	Camembert Cream
Japanese mandolin	3 large white asparagus spears
Vegetable peeler	3 tbs Chardonnay-wine vinegar
Strainer	½ cup (12 cl) apple juice
Small handheld blender	½ cup (12 cl) chicken bouillon
Nonstick baking sheet	½ cup (12 cl) heavy cream
Coffee grinder	½ Camembert
4 soup plates	2 tbs olive oil
Cruising Time	**Galley Pantry 2**
24 hours	Sweet-Sour Carrots with Cloves
	2 small baby carrots
	1 tbs rice vinegar
From the Ship's Hold	4 tbs water
Montlouis Demi-Sec	1 tbs sugar
	1 clove

April 12, 2003. Wind from the south, force 2 to 3. Clearing skies.

First Tack

The night before, prepare the sweet-sour carrots (Galley Pantry 2) and the dough for the crisps (Galley Pantry 3). For the carrots: peel and grate the carrots and place in the Mason jar. Combine the sugar, rice vinegar, water, and clove in a pot, bring to the boil, pour over the carrots. Close jar tightly and refrigerate until the next day. For the dough for the crisps: place the flour, potato flour, baking powder, salt, hazelnut oil, and water in a bowl. Blend thoroughly and refrigerate. Grind the cloves in a coffee mill. Mix this powder with the fleur de sel and set aside.

Second Tack

The next day, prepare the Camembert cream (Galley Pantry 1). Scrape the asparagus spears, chop, and sauté in the olive oil. Add the vinegar and apple juice, reduce by one-half. Add the chicken bouillon and reduce again by one-half. Next add the cream and reduce by one-fourth. Cut the top and bottom crusts off the Camembert and add the trimmed cheese to the reduced liquids. Blend this mixture and strain it. Set aside. Scrape the remaining asparagus spears (Galley Pantry 4).

Third Tack

Preheat oven to 280°F (140°C). Prepare the clove crisps (Galley Pantry 3): Knead the dough for the clove crisps. Separate the dough into a dozen strips measuring about 5–6 in. in length. Using a spoon, press the strips firmly onto a nonstick baking sheet. Sprinkle with the clove and fleur de sel mixture. Place in oven and bake for 10–12 minutes.

Landfall

Cook the white and green asparagus separately in boiling salted water. Check for doneness with the tip of a knife. Reheat the Camembert cream without boiling. Drain the sweet-sour carrots. In warmed soup plates, arrange the green asparagus on one side, the white asparagus on the other. Pour the Camembert cream in generous lines between the rows of asparagus. Place 1 tsp of the sweet-sour carrot on the edge of the plates. Sprinkle the asparagus with a few grains of the clove and fleur de sel mixture, then garnish with two clove crisps. Serve.

Cloves

Galley Pantry 3
Clove Crisps

1 tbs flour
1 tbs potato flour
1 tsp baking powder
1 pinch salt
1 tbs hazelnut oil
7 tbs water
7 cloves, ground
Fleur de sel

Galley Pantry 4
Garnish

28 firm, medium, white asparagus spears
28 firm, medium, green asparagus spears

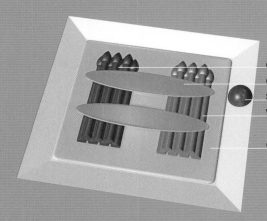

Green asparagus
Clove crisp
Sour carrot
White asparagus
Camembert cream

Setting the Course—In the old days, sailors stocked up on cider to quench their thirst during long voyages. Unlike plain water, cider did not deteriorate over time. On reaching warmer climes, however, the cider fermented and had to be consumed quickly. The ships' crews would set up huge cauldrons and brew up a special concoction containing cider, rum, and spices. Then they'd throw a party. When they returned to home port, they used the rum and spices they brought back with them to boil up another batch, in celebration of their safe journey home and the end of their sufferings at sea. They named this festive grog "Land Ahoy."

First Tack
Place the water, sugar, cider, spices, and orange and lime peels in a pot. Bring to a boil, remove from heat, and allow to steep for 4 hours. Strain and set aside.

Second Tack
Dice the pineapple. Scoop out the flesh of the passion fruit and mix with the diced pineapple.

Landfall
Place a row of licorice and another of coconut on a square saucer. Pour 1 tbs rum into each cup. Add the fruit, bring the grog to boiling point, pour into the cups.

Grog with Brittany Cider and Marie-Galante Rum

Crew of 4

Rigging
Strainer
4 coffee cups
4 saucers

Cruising Time
5 hours

Provisions

Galley Pantry 1
Grog
6 cups (1.6 liters) water
⅔ cup (200 g) light-brown sugar
1 bottle home-brewed cider
½ cinnamon stick
½ vanilla bean (pod)
½ nutmeg
½ clove
1 orange peel
1 lime peel
1½ tbs (20 g) fresh ginger

Galley Pantry 2
Garnish
1 slice fresh pineapple
1 fresh passion fruit

Galley Pantry 3
1 tsp powdered licorice
1 tsp grated coconut
4 tbs Marie-Galante rum

December 22, 2000. Force 8 gale from the west with gusting to force 9.

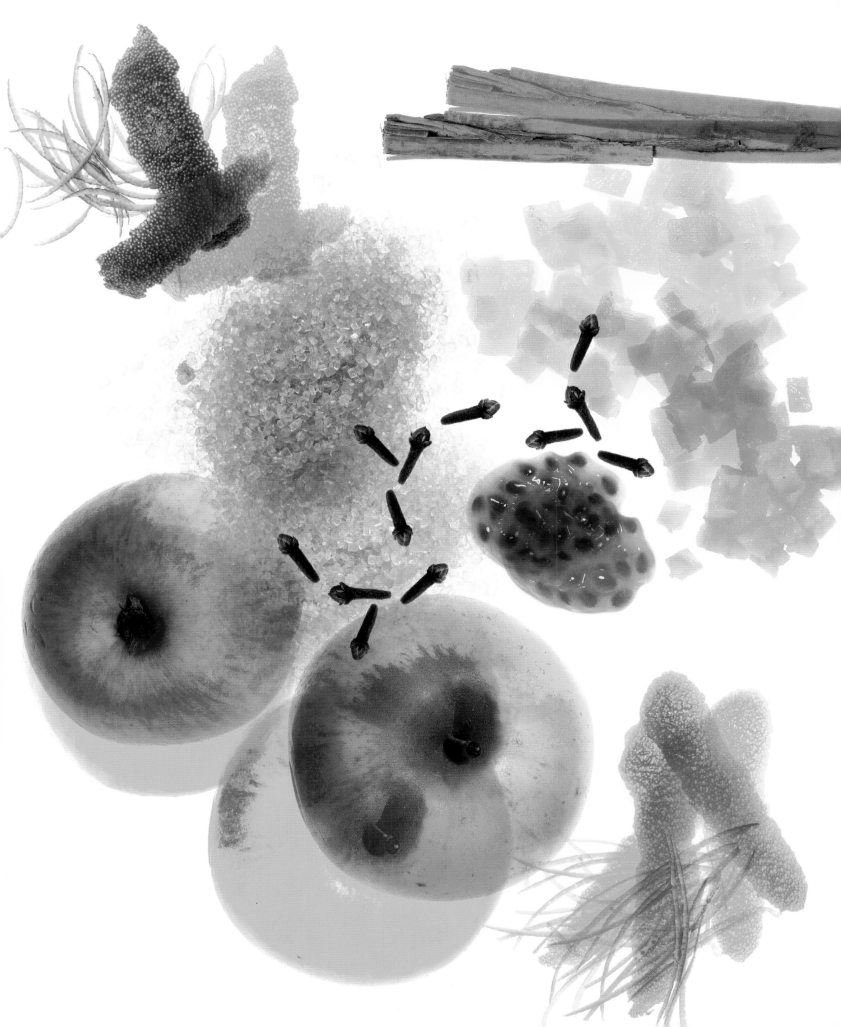

Ginger: The white spice
latitude 15°22'51" N, longitude 73°49'60" E

India. Ginger is thought to take its name from the district of Gingi, near Pondicherry in India.

History

Ginger is thought to take its name from the district of Gingi, near Pondicherry in India. Ginger comes from an elegant plant, rather like an iris, which is native to southern India. It can grow to a height of three feet (one meter). Ginger has been used in China for more than fifteen centuries. The Persians introduced ginger to Europe through their trading links with Greece, making it one of the earliest Asian spices to reach the West. For twelve centuries after that, ginger was imported into Europe by Arab merchants.

Ginger was widely used during the Middle Ages because it was much cheaper than pepper. It was especially popular in northern Europe, where it was used to flavor a wide range of dishes. When the price of pepper dropped in the course of the eighteenth century, ginger gradually fell out of fashion, except in Britain where it remained as popular as ever. In parts of Europe, ginger underwent something of a renaissance in the 1980s when chefs rediscovered its warm, peppery flavor.

Natural history

Ginger is the rhizome or underground stem of the plant *Zingiber officinale*, which is a member of the *Zingiberaceae* family.

Qualities

Ginger has a powerful taste that adds a kick to all sorts of cuisine. The first impression of fresh ginger is one of almost icy numbness. Dried ginger has a warmer, spicier taste reminiscent of pepper. Whether fresh or dry, ginger is excellent for cleaning the palate.

Uses

Ginger has long been a staple ingredient in Indian curries, Berber cuisine from North Africa, Chinese sauces, Japanese vinegar, and British beers and desserts. Today, it is used in all sorts of dishes. I like using ginger in sauces such as the stock in which I steam mussels, my nage sauce for lobsters, and fish sauces. I also find it makes excellent ice cream.

The finest ginger

The finest ginger comes from Malabar in India. I always try and get hold of pieces with three "fingers," which I find the best. The quality of the ginger depends on how the rhizome is prepared. The best ginger comes from carefully selected rhizomes that are simply peeled, washed several times, and dried. This uncoated ginger is almost white in color. I never use the more common coated ginger, where the rhizomes are not peeled but simply washed and dried, and which is grayer in color.

Health benefits

In the Middle Ages, apothecaries used ginger as a tonic, an antiseptic, and to protect against scurvy. It can also be used to treat sore throats and tonsillitis.

Setting the Course—Having become aware of its importance to our planet's future food supply, I find myself increasingly attracted by the as-yet-mysterious world of seaweed. Most people don't know it, but below the waters of Brittany lies one of the loveliest gardens in the world. It contains species that are undoubtedly unique. In this recipe, I have heightened the various flavors by combining them with ginger. The brill conserve is made by cooking the fish at a very low temperature in aromatic oil. I might mention in passing that, for fish fillets, this cooking method is my favorite.

Brill Conserve and Seaweed Broth

Crew of 4

Rigging
Terracotta baking dish, height 2 in. (5–6 cm), diameter
  8 in. (20–30 cm)
Strainer
Mason jar
Small ladle
4 soup plates

Cruising Time
24 hours

From the Ship's Hold
Châteauneuf-du-Pape or Pouilly-Fuissé

Provisions

Galley Pantry 1
1 brill weighing at least 3 lb. (1.5 kg)
3 tbs olive oil

Galley Pantry 2
Clear Broth
¼ cup (5 cl) sunflower oil
2 cloves garlic
1 knob ginger
10 tbs Japanese rice vinegar
5 tbs light soy sauce
5 tbs sesame oil
1 cup (25 cl) grape-seed oil
2 tsp sugar
1 handful dehydrated Nori seaweed

March 15, 2004. Wind from the northwest, force 4 to 5. Rough seas.

First Tack

The night before, begin preparation of the clear broth (Galley Pantry 2). Place the sunflower oil in a medium-sized saucepan and lightly sauté the peeled, chopped garlic cloves and ginger. Moisten with the Japanese rice vinegar, light soy sauce, and the sesame and grape-seed oils. Add the 2 tsp of sugar and bring to a boil. Reduce heat and simmer for 5 minutes. Remove from heat and allow to steep for 30 minutes. Strain this mixture into the Mason jar and set aside until the next day.

Second Tack

Prepare the fish (Galley Pantry 1) on the day the meal is to be served. Cut the 4 fillets from the brill and skin them. Divide the fillets into 12 even strips measuring ¾ in. wide by 3 in. long (2 x 8 cm). Set aside in the terracotta baking dish. Remove the gills from the fish head, cut the head into several pieces, place in a strainer, refrigerate.

Third Tack

Finishing preparation of the clear broth (Galley Pantry 2): After the broth has rested overnight, check the jar and note the separation of the oil at the top and the dark liquid at the bottom. Using a ladle, and taking care not to mix the two, remove the oil. Pour this oil over the fish and seal the baking dish with a sheet of aluminum foil. Set aside. Heat the olive oil in a saucepan until very hot. Plunge the fish head into the hot oil, turning until colored on both sides. Moisten with the remaining clear broth and simmer for ¾ hour. Strain, reserving the broth.

Fourth Tack

Preparing the garnish (Galley Pantry 3): Soak the dehydrated Dulse seaweed for 30 minutes in a large quantity of water. Drain, add the wine vinegar, set aside. Split the leeks in half, dice, and rinse in large quantity of water. Cook for 3 to 4 minutes in boiling salted water, refresh in ice water. Drain and place in a pot with the butter. Cut the ginger into narrow strips and add to the leeks.

Landfall

Preheat oven to 300°F (150°C). Bring the broth to boiling point. At first boil, add the handful of Nori seaweed (Galley Pantry 2). Remove from heat and steep for 10 minutes. Strain. Place the fish in the oven and bake for 12 minutes. Reheat the leeks. Warm 4 large soup plates. Arrange the fish fillets 1 in. (2.5 cm) apart in the center of each plate. Scatter the leeks between the fish fillets and sprinkle a dash of the Dulse vinegar on the tip of each fillet. Cover generously with the broth and sprinkle with a little fleur de sel (Galley Pantry 3). Serve.

Galley Pantry 3
Garnish

1 tbs dehydrated Dulse seaweed
1 tbs red-wine vinegar
4 small leeks
1 tbs (10 g) lightly salted butter
5 strips ginger preserved in vinegar
Fleur de sel

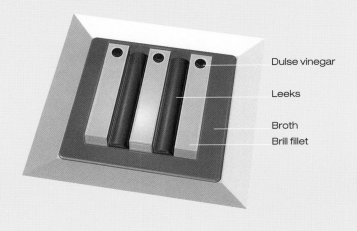

Dulse vinegar

Leeks

Broth
Brill fillet

Setting the Course—This recipe has become a classic at Les Maisons de Bricourt, and that is because it's emblematic—and perhaps even the source—of the long route my cuisine has followed. It also reflects my original love affair with ground spices, fish, and history. It is said that in the eighteenth century, fourteen spices were stored behind the protective ramparts of Saint-Malo. These are the very spices I use in this recipe. Could the gentlemen of Saint-Malo—wealthy shipbuilders who reveled in their vessels' aromatic holds—have invented this dish? Were they familiar with the perfect marriage between the flesh of this princely denizen of the sea and their own world of imported spices? Probably not, but I like to think they were, and to dream of the epic voyage taken by the spices from their own distant and fragrant lands to the rockbound coast of my own region. My "Voyage from the Indies" actually starts right here at home.

John Dory, or the Voyage from the

Crew of 4

Rigging
Steam cooker
Strainer
Mortar
Coffee mill
4 plates

Cruising Time
2 days

From the Ship's Hold
Vouvray Demi-Sec or
   Gewürztraminer

Provisions

Galley Pantry 1
1 Dory weighing 3–4 lb. (1.6 kg to
   2 kg). Ask your fish seller to
   remove the fillets from the whole
   fish. Keep the bones for fish
   stock.

Galley Pantry 2
1 onion
1 large knob ginger (equal to
   two ordinary knobs)
¾ cup (20 cl) fish stock
1 stick citronella
2 tbs (20 g) + 2 tbs (20 g) butter
1 clove garlic

Galley Pantry 3
3 tbs sugar
1 tsp cardamom
5 tbs rice vinegar
¾ cup (20 cl) chicken bouillon

Galley Pantry 4
3 sprigs mint
3 sprigs coriander
5 tbs coconut milk

Galley Pantry 5
"Voyage to the Indies" Powder
This mixture is available ready-to-use at
Les Maisons de Bricourt (see Poudre
Retour des Indes, page 234). Proportions
will vary depending on the quality and
origin of each spice.
1 tsp mace
½ Chinese anise
½ tsp black pepper
1 tsp dried coriander seeds

April 17, 1990. Wind from the east, force 4 to 5. Nice brisk breeze.

First Tack

Forty-eight hours before serving, prepare the "Voyage From the Indies" powder (Galley Pantry 5). In a large dry frying pan, heat all the spices listed under Galley Pantry 5 except the vanilla, turmeric, Cayenne pepper, and dried lily petals. When these ingredients reach the fragrance point, add the remaining spices and pulverize in a coffee mill. Set aside.

Second Tack

Twenty-four hours before serving, prepare the sauce (Galley Pantry 2). Chop the peeled onion and ginger coarsely and sauté in the first part of the butter. Add 1 tbs of the spice mixture and heat quickly. Add the fish stock and simmer for 30 minutes. Add the chopped citronella and whole peeled garlic clove. Set aside. Continue preparation of the sauce (Galley Pantry 3). Crush the cardamom in a mortar. Heat the sugar in a dry frying pan, stirring constantly until it caramelizes. When the sugar is a pale brown color, add the cardamom. Add the vinegar to arrest the cooking process. The caramel will bubble and spit when the vinegar is added, so great care should be taken during this step. Add the chicken bouillon, stir to blend, simmer 30 minutes, remove from heat. Combine the ingredients listed under Galley Pantries 2 and 3 and add to the ingredients listed under Galley Pantry 4. Allow to steep until the following day (minimum 12 hours).

Third Tack

On the day the meal is to be served, prepare the garnishes (Galley Pantry 6). Make a compote with the apples and mangos. Dice, combine, and cook uncovered for about 10 minutes, stirring constantly. The fruit should form a thick purée. Set aside in the pot. Sort, wash, and drain the garden cress. Tear the leaves off the cabbage, cut out the ribs and discard. Chop the trimmed leaves.

Cook the cabbage rapidly in boiling salted water and refresh in ice water. Set aside in a pot with 1 tbs water. Chop the fresh peeled turmeric (use gloves, as turmeric stains). Parboil, drain, and refresh. Follow the same procedure with the ginger. Dice the pear, add the lemon juice. Combine the pear, ginger, and turmeric.

Fourth Tack

Divide the fish fillets (Galley Pantry 1). Each half of the Dory can be separated into three fillets. Cut the largest fillet into 3 equal pieces and the medium fillet into 2 equal pieces. Leave the third fillet whole. Set aside. Strain the sauce from Galley Pantries 2, 3, and 4, pressing well to extract the juice. Set aside.

Landfall

Cook the fish fillets for 5 minutes in the steam cooker. Reheat the fruit compote and the cabbage. Heat the sauce, without boiling, and add the remaining 2 tbs (20 g) butter (Galley Pantry 2). Arrange the cabbage on one side of the serving plate, the garden cress on the other. Place one fish fillet on the cabbage, one fillet between the two vegetables, and the last fillet on the cress. Top each fillet with a bit of the turmeric-pear-ginger mixture. Place an oblong of the fruit compote on the edge of the plate. Garnish with a few leaves of coriander. Pour the sauce around the fillets on the cabbage. Serve.

Indies. . .

½ tsp toasted caraway seeds
½ tbs Szechuan pepper
½ tsp bitter-orange peel
1 clove
½ inch (1 cm) cinnamon stick
½ vanilla bean (pod)
2 tsp ground turmeric
1 dash Cayenne pepper
1 tsp dried lily petals

Galley Pantry 6
Garnishes

2 mangos
1 apple
1 handful garden cress
1 spring cabbage

Finishing the Dory

1 small knob fresh turmeric (size of a walnut, approx.)
1 small knob fresh ginger (size of a walnut, approx.)
¼ pear + dash of lemon juice
2 sprigs fresh coriander

Compote
Turmeric-pear-ginger mixture
Garden cress
John Dory

Cabbage sauce

Setting the Course—The rust-colored rock clam is notable for its unusual jagged shape. The peppery tang and organic liquor of this elusive treat have found a home for themselves in Brittany. Perhaps this shellfish should be dubbed the "Shanghaied" clam, in memory of the youthful mariners who were kidnapped ("shanghaied") and shipped on voyages around the Horn. They returned via Chile, the route taken by gold-seekers, and often sailed again to the ends of the earth on whalers, sometimes finishing their days in the gambling dens of Shanghai. In my recipe, these travels are evoked by the ginger and Chinese cabbage, which afford an unexpected tang to the clams.

Clams, Pickled Ginger, and Chinese

Crew of 4

Rigging
Small rigid knife for opening the clams
Strainer
24 small sake bowls

Cruising Time
1 hour

From the Ship's Hold
Château-Grillet or Hermitage Blanc

Provisions

Galley Pantry 1
24 large clams

Galley Pantry 2
Garnish
12 leaves Chinese cabbage (approx. half a cabbage)
3 tbs olive oil

October 20, 2003. Wind from the southwest, force 5 to 6 with gusts force 6 to 7. Rough seas, swirling mist, poor visibility.

First Tack

The clams (Galley Pantry 1): Open the clams, remove from shells. Strain the liquor. Set aside ⅓ of the strained liquor for the sauce. Place the shelled clams in a pot with the remaining liquor. Set aside.

Second Tack

Garnish (Galley Pantry 2): Chop the cabbage leaves, set aside.

Third Tack

Sauce (Galley Pantry 3): Peel and chop the shallot, transfer to a saucepan with the 3 tbs Chardonnay white-wine vinegar. Bring to a boil and reduce until the vinegar has completely evaporated. Remove three strips of rind from the orange. Squeeze the orange, set the juice aside. Peel and chop the ginger. Pour the clam liquor and orange juice onto the pickled shallot. Add the orange rind and chopped ginger. Bring to a boil and reduce by one-third. Strain. Chop the ginger preserved in vinegar, add to the sauce. Set these ingredients aside in a pot.

Landfall

Briefly sauté the chopped cabbage leaves (Galley Pantry 2) with the olive oil in a large frying pan, as you would in a wok. Cube the butter (Gally Pantry 3), add to the sauce, and bring to a boil. Warm the clams in their liquor. Arrange the chopped cabbage leaves in sake bowls (six bowls per person) and top with one drained warm clam per bowl. Finish with the sauce, dividing the ginger equally among the bowls. Serve.

Cabbage

Galley Pantry 3
Sauce

1 large shallot
3 tbs white-wine vinegar (Chardonnay or Champagne)
1 orange
1 knob fresh ginger
⅓ of the clam liquor
1 tbs (20 g) ginger preserved in vinegar (available at
   Asian groceries)
6 tbs (100 g) butter

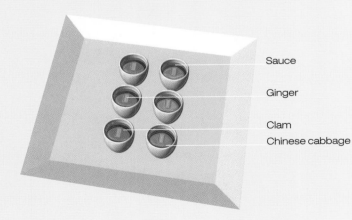

Sauce

Ginger

Clam
Chinese cabbage

Setting the Course—Scooping up a warm spoonful of pear is a marvelous way to absorb the last warmth of summer's sun, a sensual treat before "battening down" for winter. When the generous luxury of praline and the spicy bite of ginger are added, this rare moment is enhanced by the unique impression afforded by the meeting of two parallel worlds.

Preserved Pear with Hazelnut Praline

Crew of 4

Rigging
Japanese mandolin
Sorbet maker
Apple-corer, vegetable-scraper
Cake rack
Nonstick baking sheet
Bowl
Strainer
Pastry brush
Small handheld blender
4 plates

Cruising Time
6 hours

From the Ship's Hold
A mellow Vouvray

Provisions

Galley Pantry 1
Praline
1 ½ oz. (50 g) milk chocolate
⅔ cup (150 g) praline
¼ cup (75 g) feuilletine (available at specialty groceries)

Galley Pantry 2
Ginger Ice Cream
¼ cup (scant 50 g) fresh peeled ginger
¼ cup (scant 50 g) preserved ginger
¼ cup (60 g) sugar + ¼ cup (scant 50 g) sugar
2 cups (50 cl) milk
⅔ cup (150 g) cream
6 egg yolks

October 4, 2003. Very rough seas.

First Tack

Feuilletine Praline (Galley Pantry 1): Melt the milk chocolate in a double-boiler, remove from heat, and cool to lukewarm. Mix the praline and the feuilletine together in a bowl, add the lukewarm chocolate and stir until well blended. Set aside.

Second Tack

Ginger ice cream (Galley Pantry 2): Blanche the fresh ginger twice, drain, and combine with the preserved ginger and sugar. Bring the milk, cream, and half the remaining sugar to a boil. Combine the egg yolks with the other half of the remaining sugar and beat until light. Add the ginger mixture to the hot milk and steep for 15 minutes. Strain. Reheat the milk, add the egg mixture, and finish as for custard sauce. Place in the sorbet maker and store in freezer.

Third Tack

Poached pear (Galley Pantry 3): Peel the pears with a vegetable-scraper and then core them. Prepare a syrup with the water, sugar, and lemon juice. Bring to the boil, add the pears. Cover with a clean cloth and simmer for 10 minutes. Check for doneness with the tip of a knife. Remove the pears from the heat and allow to finish cooking for a few moments in the hot syrup. Transfer the cooked pears to a cake rack.

Fourth Tack

Pear petals (Galley Pantry 4): Make a syrup with the water, sugar, and lemon juice. Peel and core the pears, slice with a Japanese mandolin. Add the pear slices to the hot syrup and allow to stand for 30 minutes. Drain the pear slices, place on a nonstick baking sheet and bake very slowly at 175°F (80°C) for 2 hours. Cool and store in an airtight container.

Fifth Tack

Caramel sauce (Galley Pantry 5): Melt the sugar in a dry pan and allow to caramelize, stirring constantly. Heat the light cream and pour it carefully onto the caramel to deglaze the pan.

Landfall

Pour two rows of caramel sauce onto the left-hand side of four medium-sized plates. Fill the poached pears with praline. Warm slightly in oven. Arrange the filled pears on the serving plates; cover with caramel sauce. Place three pear petals around each filled pear and garnish with an oblong of ginger ice cream on the side.

Ginger Flavoring

Galley Pantry 3
Poached Pears
4 pears (Conference or early Barletts)
1 ½ cups (40 cl) water
1 cup (300 g) sugar
4 tbs lemon juice

Galley Pantry 4
Pear Petals
2 pears (Conference or early Bartletts)
½ cup (10 cl) water
½ cup (125 g) sugar
2 tbs lemon juice

Galley Pantry 5
Caramel Sauce
¼ cup (50 g) sugar
¼ cup (50 g) light cream

Pear with praline
Pear petal

Caramel sauce

Ginger ice cream

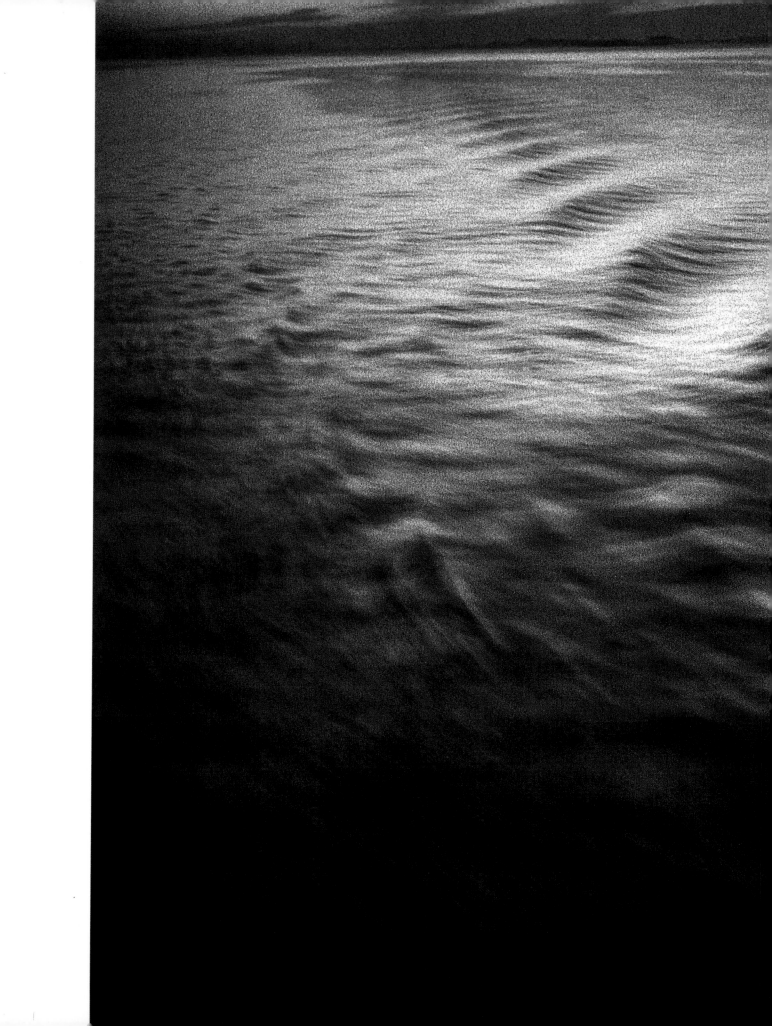

Cinnamon: Ineffably suave
latitude 7°15′ N, longitude 78°32′ E

Sri Lanka. Like the Greeks and the Romans, the Crusaders were convinced of the truth of a host of legends purporting to explain the origins of this delicately perfumed wood. Some believed it grew in the realm of the Queen of Sheba, others that it was found only in some forgotten earthly Garden of Eden.

History

Like the Greeks and the Romans, the Crusaders were convinced of the truth of a host of legends purporting to explain the origins of this delicately perfumed wood. Some believed it grew in the realm of the Queen of Sheba, others that it was found only in some forgotten earthly Garden of Eden. The Egyptian traders who made their fortune dealing in cinnamon were instrumental in spreading these tales, as a way of justifying the exorbitant prices they demanded for their precious cargo. While the old legends are no longer taken seriously, it is true that cinnamon did come from a far-distant land that has some claim to be called an earthly paradise.

It was only in 1505, when the Portuguese arrived in Ceylon—now Sri Lanka—that they discovered the home of cinnamon. They were soon replaced by the Dutch, who handed control of the production of this precious spice to the Dutch East India Company, thus guaranteeing a monopoly that lasted until the end of the eighteenth century, when the extremely lucrative trade passed into the hands of the English.

In ancient China, cinnamon was a symbol of poetry. The Hebrews used it in their sacred oils. In Rome, it was synonymous with extravagance and luxury. For centuries, Arab traders and Venetian doges who controlled the supply to Europe made fortunes from cinnamon. It is said that, after months at sea, sailors knew when they were approaching the island of Ceylon because the scent of cinnamon wafted dozens of miles out to sea. I wish I could have lived such a magical moment. I love these bits of perfumed tree bark from across the seas.

Natural history

True cinnamon, which is the bark of the young shoots of *Cinnamomum zeylanicum*, a large tree of the *Lauraceae* family, should not be confused with cassia or Chinese cinnamon, *Cinnamomum cassia*, which is less subtle. They can be told apart by the thickness and color of the bark. Cinnamon is thinner and is a warm yellow-brown, while cassia is thicker and almost gray in color.

Qualities

Ceylon cinnamon contains a cinnamic acid that gives it a deep yet refined flavor. True cinnamon has a very characteristic taste, which is pleasant, warm, and intense.

Uses

Cinnamon is the second most widely used spice, after pepper. It is used in all sorts of culinary traditions, from the Five Spices mix used in Chinese cookery and the Indian garam masala, to typically English puddings and crumbles. Its intense, warming flavor explains why it is so popular in the chilly climates of northern Europe. I use cinnamon in all sorts of dishes. It brings a charming rounded note to fruit, particularly citrus fruit. But it is at its finest when married with chocolate.

The finest cinnamon

Without a doubt, the finest cinnamon in the world comes from Sri Lanka.

Health benefits

Because it stimulates the sweat glands and contains the essential oil cinnamic aldehyde, cinnamon helps treat coughs, colds, and influenza. It is also a good remedy against general fatigue.

Setting the Course—This improbable combination of foie gras, fish, and melon is ideal with the Venetian Serinissima powder. I once read that this powder was already used in the Middle Ages. But it was when I added the Port—a wine traditionally aged in ships' holds—that I dared combine the musky flavor of foie gras, the clam-like flesh of sea bream, and the suave touch afforded by the "petit gris" melon from Rennes. What really ties it all together, perhaps, is the mint. . . .

Cubes of Foie Gras and Sea Bream, Me

Crew of Four

Rigging
4 pastry molds, 1½ in. (4 cm) high and 2½ in.
  (6 cm) in diameter
Strainer
Small handheld blender
Coffee mill
4 soup plates

Cruising Time
24 hours

From the Ship's Hold
10-year old Tawny Port

Provisions

Galley Pantry 1
½ "petit gris" melon from Rennes
1 fillet of sea bream weighing 5 oz. (150 g), prepared by
  your fish seller
5 oz. (150 g) foie gras cooked in a terrine

Galley Pantry 2
Serinissima Powder
This may be purchased "ready-to-use" at Les Maisons de Bricourt
(see Poudre Serinissima, page 234). It is difficult to specify the exact
proportions of this mixture, since it can vary depending on the origin
and quality of the spices used.
2 sticks cinnamon
½ tsp Guinea pepper
1 tsp coriander seeds
2 cloves
1 tsp ground nutmeg
1 tsp dried ground ginger
1 dash ground saffron
1 tsp muscovado sugar

July 4, 2002. Clear weather, east wind force 2 to 3. Sparkling sea.

First Tack

Begin with the Serinissima powder (Galley Pantry 2). Crush the cinnamon stick and pulverize in the coffee grinder with the Guinea pepper, coriander seeds, and cloves. Add the ground nutmeg, ginger, saffron, and sugar. Mix together and set aside.

Second Tack

Marinade (Galley Pantry 3): Prepare the night before. Combine all the ingredients—the white Chardonnay or Champagne vinegar, soy sauce, almond oil, sunflower oil, orange juice, and fresh peeled and chopped ginger. Blend with small handheld blender and set aside overnight.

Third Tack

The Port wine syrup (Galley Pantry 4): Allow approximately 2 hours for reduction of the syrup. Place the Port, sugar, 3 fresh tomatoes (skinned and chopped), and Serinissima powder in a pan. Bring to a boil, reduce heat and simmer until reduced to two-thirds of original volume. Blend with small handheld blender, strain. Reduce again, this time by half. Set aside.

Fourth Tack

A few hours before serving, scoop out the pulp of the melon, mash with a fork, and set aside in a strainer. Cut the sea bream fillet and foie gras into small cubes. Set aside 4 almond halves and chop the rest. Set aside 4 small mint leaves and chop the rest.

Landfall

Twenty minutes before serving, whip the marinade vigorously. Place the cubes of sea bream and foie gras in a bowl, cover with the marinade, steep for 15 minutes. Drain. Place one pastry mold on each of 4 soup plates and fill with this mixture. Mix the chopped mint and melon pulp, spread around the outside of the molds. Add the chopped almonds. Remove the molds and garnish the finished dish with half an almond and a small mint leaf. Moisten with two splashes of Port wine syrup. Serve.

on and Port Wine with Serinissima Powder

Galley Pantry 3
Marinade

3 tbs Chardonnay Blanc wine vinegar (or Champagne vinegar)
2 tbs soy sauce
5 tbs almond oil
4 tbs sunflower oil
Juice of 1 orange
1 knob fresh ginger

Galley Pantry 4
Port Wine Syrup

1 bottle Tawny Port
1 tbs sugar
3 fresh tomatoes
Serinissima powder (Galley Pantry 2)

Finishing
8 fresh almonds
8 small leaves mint

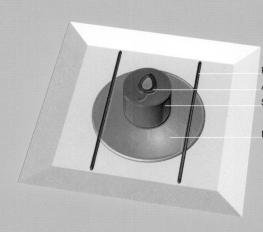

Port wine syrup
Almond and mint leaf
Sea bream and foie gras

Melon pulp

Setting the Course—Young mariners from Brittany once sailed regularly to Shanghai—not in search of cinnamon, of course, but of whales. When I was a teenager, I was obsessed by tales of faraway places like China. And later, when I began to study the science and alchemy of stocks, I decided to do some exploring of my own. It was my "China dream" that led me to add an exotic touch to our native spider crabs, the flesh of which is particularly delicate when lukewarm. My youthful dreams would be fully realized if I could serve this dish on one of those East India Company willowware platters with wavy vermeil varnish.

Shanghai-Style Bouillon for Spider Crab

Crew of Four

Rigging
Small handheld blender
12 stainless-steel discs or plastic tubes measuring 1 ¼ in.
  (3 cm) in diameter and 1 ½ in. (4 cm) in height
Strainer
Grater with small holes
4 soup plates

Cruising Time
4 hours

From the Ship's Hold
Montlouis Sec

Provisions

Galley Pantry 1
4 spider crabs weighing 2 lbs. (1 kg) each, preferably
  2 males and 2 females (the males are easier to shell,
  the females often contain more coral)
10 quarts water + ½ lb. (200 g) coarse salt +
  1 tsp Cayenne pepper

Galley Pantry 2
Shanghai Bouillon
¼ lb. (100 g) shrimps
1 cup cooking liquid from the spider crabs
1 cup water
½ tsp honey
½ tsp nuoc-mâm
Dash of Cayenne pepper
1 stick citronella
2 cumbava leaves
1 tsp green tea
½ stick cinnamon

July 2, 2004. Wind from northeast, force 3 to 4. Pleasant breeze.

First Tack
Cooking the spider crabs (Galley Pantry 1): Plunge the shellfish in 10 quarts of boiling water seasoned with the salt and Cayenne pepper. When the water returns to the boil, continue cooking for 20 minutes. Remove the shellfish and allow to cool. Cut open the heads, extract the coral and gray matter, set aside. Carefully shell the bodies and claws. Set aside.

Second Tack
Coraline vinaigrette (Galley Pantry 3): Add 2 tbs of the reserved coral to the vinaigrette ingredients (Galley Pantry 3). For the coral canapés: place the remaining coral, crème fraîche, and butter in a small pan. Heat slowly and simmer for 3 minutes, stirring constantly. Blend (using hand blender) and press through a strainer. Refrigerate. Toast the slices of bread and cut into 12 small squares. Set aside.

Third Tack
Shanghai bouillon (Galley Pantry 2): Strain 1 cup of the shellfish cooking liquid into a pot. Add 1 cup water and the shrimps. Bring to a boil, reduce heat, and simmer for 15 minutes. Add the honey, nuoc-mâm, Cayenne pepper, stick of citronella, chopped cumbava leaves, green tea, and cinnamon. Bring to boil and remove from heat. Cover and allow to infuse for 30 minutes. Strain and set aside.

Fourth Tack
Garnishes (Galley Pantry 4): Grate the green mango. Chop the spring onions. Cut the carrot into small matchsticks.

Landfall
Toast the squares of bread on one side, spread the untoasted side with the coral cream. Place three of the stainless-steel discs or plastic tubes in each of four soup plates. Season the crabmeat with the vinaigrette and reheat in a pan. Arrange the warm meat inside the three discs in each soup plate, pressing down lightly. Reheat the bouillon and pour into a carafe. Remove the discs. Place one leaf of lemon balm on each mound of crabmeat. Serve. Pour the bouillon into the soup plates at the table.

Galley Pantry 3
Coraline Vinaigrette
⅓ cup (100 g) sunflower oil
¼ tsp Dijon mustard
1 tbs sherry vinegar
Dash of Tabasco sauce
10 leaves flat parsley
Salt, pepper

Coral Canapés
Coral from 2 female spider crabs
1 tbs crème fraîche
1 tbs (20g) butter
2 slices wholemeal bread

Galley Pantry 4
Garnish
¼ green mango
4 spring onions
1 carrot
4 leaves lemon balm

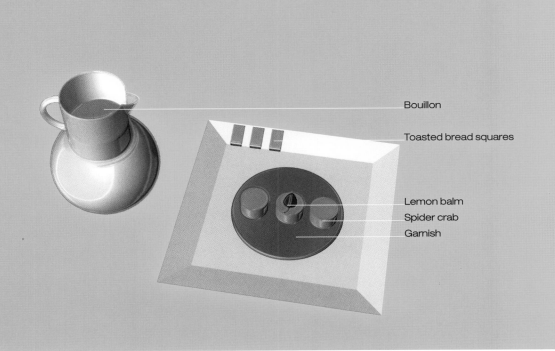

Bouillon
Toasted bread squares
Lemon balm
Spider crab
Garnish

Setting the Course—Cinnamon and chocolate are a marriage made in heaven; a classic combination, but one that never ceases to thrill me. When I embark on this journey, I unite two rare staples with disparate origins. One comes from the New World, shimmering on the far horizon; the other from the deserts and mountains of China. To underscore the delicacy of the cinnamon and purity of the chocolate, I've added the crisp and crunchy texture of coarsely chopped nougatine. But there's something else—the coconut pearl tapioca: final affirmation of an exotic world that is light, so light. . . .

Cinnamon Parfait, Chocolate Sorbet

74

Crew of Four

Rigging
5 stainless-steel discs ½ in. (1.5 cm) high, 4 in. (9.5 cm)
    in diameter
Strainer
Pastry bag with plain tip ½ in. (12 mm) in diameter
Small "Kitchenaid"-type blender
Nonstick baking sheet
Candy thermometer
Sorbet maker
4 soup plates

Cruising Time
24 hours

From the Ship's Hold
Banyuls or Maury

Provisions

Galley Pantry 1
Cinnamon Parfait
3 tsp freshly-ground cinnamon
6 egg yolks
2 tbs water
7 tbs sugar
¾ cup (180 g) heavy cream, whipped

Galley Pantry 2
Pearls of Japan
½ cup (125 g) + ½ cup (125 g) milk
2 tsp sugar
Rind of ¼ orange
3 tsp Japanese pearl tapioca (available at Japanese
    groceries)
¼ cup (50 g) heavy cream
½ cup (125 g) puréed coconut

March 15, 2003. Wind from the south, force 4 to 5. Rough, choppy sea.

First Tack

Cinnamon parfait (Galley Pantry 1): Add the ground cinnamon to the egg yolks and beat for 10 minutes. Bring the water and sugar to a boil and continue cooking until the mixture reaches a temperature of 250°F (121°C). Meanwhile, beat the cream with a wire whisk until stiff. When the sugar syrup has attained the correct temperature, gently stir in the egg yolk and ground cinnamon mixture. Allow to cool and fold in the whipped cream. Fill the stainless-steel discs with this mixture. Store in freezer.

Second Tack

Pearls of Japan (Galley Pantry 2): Place the milk, sugar, and orange peel in a pot. Bring to the boil. Add the pearl tapioca and simmer, stirring constantly, until the pearls are translucent Remove from heat, cool, and add the rest of the milk, heavy cream, and puréed coconut.

Third Tack

Chocolate sorbet (Galley Pantry 3): Break the chocolate into pieces and place in a bowl with the powdered cocoa. Heat the milk and sugar to boiling point. Pour the hot milk onto the chocolate mixture. Mix thoroughly and strain. Transfer to the sorbet maker, place in freezer.

Fourth Tack

Preheat oven to 325°F (165°C). Place the almonds, hazelnuts, and pistachios (Galley Pantry 4) on a baking sheet and toast in the oven until brown. Place the sugar and water in a copper pan, bring to boil and continue cooking until a temperature of 230°F (110°C) is reached. Add the toasted nuts. Remove from heat and stir until the sugar whitens slightly. Return to heat, stirring, and allow to caramelize. Pour onto a nonstick baking sheet and cool. Pry the caramelized nuts off the baking sheet and crush. Store in an airtight tin.

Landfall

Prepare 4 large soup plates. Place a disc containing the frozen parfait in the center of each plate. Place another disc over the parfait and add the nuts. Gently remove both discs from the plates. Garnish with the coconut milk and the pearl tapioca. To finish, top with an oblong of chocolate sorbet. Serve.

and Coconut Pearl Tapioca

Galley Pantry 3
Chocolate Sorbet

1 ½ oz. dark chocolate (66% cacao)
4 tbs powdered cocoa
1 cup (250 g) milk
4 tbs sugar

Galley Pantry 4

3 tbs whole unskinned almonds
3 tbs whole skinned hazelnuts
4 tbs whole green pistachios
3 tbs water
3 tsp sugar

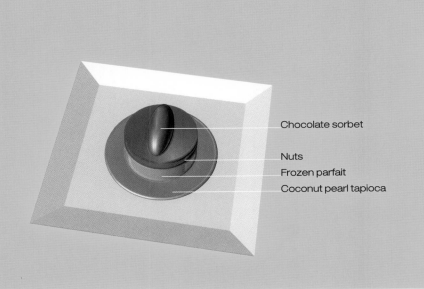

Chocolate sorbet

Nuts
Frozen parfait
Coconut pearl tapioca

Cumin: The universal spice
latitude 35°53'59" N, longitude 14°30'53" E

Malta. According to legend, cumin is native to the island of Comino, northeast of Malta.

History

According to legend, cumin is native to the island of Comino, northeast of Malta. The Hebrew origin of the name, however, suggests that it originated in the Middle East. It is mentioned in the Bible as a plant cultivated in gardens. Archaeologists have also found evidence of cumin cultivation in the Nile valley. The Romans used cumin lavishly for their feasts. From there, the spice spread to the Arab world, where it has remained popular ever since. As the Arab conquests expanded their sphere of influence to the east, cumin reached India and Indonesia towards the end of the first millennium C.E. The Crusaders brought cumin back with them from the Middle East. It was extremely popular in Spain, and ships setting sail for the New World would fill their holds with cumin.

Natural history

The brown-gray elongated seeds of the plant *Cuminum cyminum* are no more than ¼ inch (6 mm) long. The seeds of *Cuminum cyminum*, a small annual, are dried in the sun. Be careful not to confuse cumin and caraway, which is similar in taste; both plants belong to the *Umbellifera* family. The way to tell them apart is that cumin is lighter in color and has a line down the center of the seed dividing it into two halves, whereas caraway is one single seed.

Qualities

Cumin has an unusual, powerful, peppery flavor, but its aroma is more pungent than its taste. It is warming on the palate, slightly bitter and piquant. Whenever I hear the word cumin, I can smell the trade winds laden with the exotic aroma of the spice. The scent of cumin is the scent of adventure. The intense, dry heat of the taste is the taste of the desert.

Uses

Cumin is used in all the world cuisines that have a reputation for fiery tastes, such as Indian curries and garam masala. It is a key ingredient in the spice mixes that give the cuisine of North Africa and the Middle East their rich flavor, and is even used in Spanish and Mexican cooking. Traditional European cooking uses more caraway than cumin, in cakes, biscuits, and cheese.

I often dry-fry a few seeds in a pan before use, to bring out the full aroma and flavor. Cumin always goes extremely well with mint and is delicious mixed with some plain yogurt or fromage blanc as a sauce for salads. A few cumin seeds scattered over oven-cooked fish marry with the juices to create a marvelous fragrant steam. Paprika and cumin together are excellent with butternut squash soup and with a purée of carrots and potatoes.

Caraway is better than cumin with cheeses such as Munster.

Cumin brings balance to a number of world cuisines.

The finest cumin

The finest cumin is grown in northwest India, particularly in Rajasthan. Moroccan cumin is also of outstanding quality.

Good-quality cumin has well-defined seeds with a tiny stalk. Never buy ready-ground cumin, which will have lost all its flavor before you even get home.

Health benefits

Modern research has shown cumin to have anti-spasmodic qualities, and to be good for the stomach. It is also recommended as an herbal tea to counter flatulence. Indians use cumin to treat indigestion.

Setting the Course—I once found myself seated at dawn in the stern of a boat pulling slowly away from the Indian port of Cochin. There was a light mist. To starboard lay a shadowy filigree of Chinese nets. As the water rustled gently along the keel of the boat, I seemed to be floating back in time. Cochin, an open gateway to the East, has seen everything: migrating Jews in the fourth century; Portuguese, Dutch, English, and French explorers, ambitious Arab merchants and mariners. The only traces remaining of this restless activity are the synagogue and the moss-covered grave of Vasco da Gama. But the fragrance of the local spices is unchanged—stronger here, perhaps, than anywhere else in the world. I should also mention the Indian method for transforming milk. This yogurt-like concoction continues to stupefy me.

Scallops with Fleur de Sel, Yogurt, and

Crew of 4	Provisions
Rigging	**Galley Pantry 1**
Baking dish	16 large scallops
Coffee mill	½ lb. (200 g) coarse salt
Small handheld blender	
Strainer	**Marinade**
4 plates	1 cup (25 cl) water
	5 tbs rice vinegar
Cruising Time	7 tbs sugar
6 hours	½ lemon
From the Ship's Hold	**Galley Pantry 2**
Saint-Véran	**"Rêve de Cochin" Powder**
	This blend is available ready-to-use from Les Maisons de Bricourt
	(see page 234). The proportions given are a guide only.
	1 nutmeg
	1 tbs coriander seeds
	1 tbs cumin seeds
	1 tbs green anise seeds
	½ tbs green cardamom pods
	1 tbs black peppercorns

October 15, 1999. Mild wind from the east, force 2 to 3. Almost cloudless sky.

First Tack

At least six hours before serving, remove the scallops from their shells (Galley Pantry 1), or ask your fish seller to do it for you. Rinse the scallops well, dredge in coarse salt, allow to stand for three hours, and then soak in fresh water for one hour to remove the salt.

Second Tack

Meanwhile, prepare the "Rêve de Cochin" powder (Galley Pantry 2). Crush the nutmeg and place with all the other spices in the coffee mill. Pulverize and set aside. Next, prepare the scallop marinade (Galley Pantry 1). In a receptacle large enough to hold the scallops, combine the water, rice vinegar, sugar, and lemon juice. Stir until the sugar is dissolved. Set aside.

Third Tack

Fruit vinaigrette (Galley Pantry 3): In a large bowl, combine the mango flesh with the almond and grape-seed oils. Place the flesh and seeds of the passion fruit in a pot and add the pineapple juice, Cayenne pepper, saffron, and chopped citronella. Blend thoroughly with handheld blender. Strain and set aside.

Fourth Tack

Finish the scallops. Steep the desalted scallops in the marinade for 1½ hours, drain, and set aside. Prepare the Cochin sauce (Galley Pantry 2). Combine 1 tsp "Rêve de Cochin" powder with the yogurt, refrigerate, and allow to steep for 30 minutes. Strain.

Landfall

Slice each of the scallops into 4 or 5 rounds. Transfer to a plate, cover with the vinegar, and marinate for 5 minutes. Arrange 5 to 6 scallop slices in three rows on each of the four serving plates. Pour the Cochin-and-yogurt sauce between the rows. Serve.

"Rêve de Cochin" Powder

Cochin Sauce
1 yogurt
1 tsp "Rêve de Cochin" powder

Galley Pantry 3
Fruit Vinaigrette
1 mango (⅓ cup or 100 g of flesh)
2 tbs almond oil
6 tbs grape-seed oil
3 passion fruit
10 tbs pineapple juice
¼ stick citronella
1 dash Cayenne pepper
3 saffron pistils

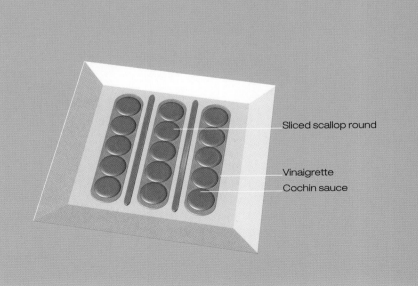

Sliced scallop round

Vinaigrette
Cochin sauce

Setting the Course—For me, all the flavor of the sea is concentrated in this tender silver-blue flesh accented with "cuminized" mustard and seaweed. Mackerel is probably the only fish that is perfect just as it is, raw or cooked. My mackerel is caught by an old fisherman friend of mine. A retired sea-dog of the old school, he knows all the tricks of the trade and is never happier than when he's out in his boat. Skinning raw mackerel can be a problem, however. I use a special technique to prize off the tough "snakeskin," and take great pleasure in admiring the iridescent patterns of the glistening fish while I'm doing it.

Silvery Raw Mackerel with Celtic

Crew of 4

Rigging
Coffee mill
Kitchen shears
Box of small wooden toothpicks
Mason jar
4 small sake bowls
4 plates

Cruising Time
6 hours

From the Ship's Hold
Pouilly-Fumé or Sancerre Blanc

Provisions

Galley Pantry 1
6 whole mackerel weighing ¾ lb. (300 g) each
3 tbs (50 g) salt

Galley Pantry 2
Sweet-Sour Marinade
½ cup (10 cl) water
1 cup (20 cl) rice vinegar
1 lemon
3 tbs sugar
1 tbs cumin seeds

July 3, 2001. Wind from the north, force 1 to 2. Clear weather; calm sea.

First Tack

Preparing the mackerel (Galley Pantry 1): Remove the fillets from the whole fish. Salt the fillets on both sides, place on a plate without overlapping, and refrigerate for 3 hours. Soak in a large amount of water for 1 hour in order to remove the salt. Drain.

Second Tack

Prepare the marinades (Galley Pantries 2 and 3). Start with the sweet-sour marinade (Galley Pantry 2). Combine the water, rice vinegar, lemon juice, 3 tbs sugar, and 1 tbs cumin seeds. Stir until the sugar has completely dissolved. Place the mackerel fillets in the marinade, refrigerate for 1½ hours, then drain. Remove the bones and the thin transparent membrane. Next, prepare the citrus-soy marinade (Galley Pantry 3). Peel and crush the garlic clove. Peel and chop the ginger. Place the garlic, ginger, orange juice, lemon juice, soy sauce, grape-seed and almond oils in the Mason jar. Close the jar tightly, shake vigorously, and refrigerate

Third Tack

Celtic marine mustard (Galley Pantry 4): Heat the cumin seeds in a dry saucepan. When they are lightly colored, transfer to the coffee mill. Use shears to cut the Nori leaves, add them to the cumin seeds in the coffee mill. Pulverize these two ingredients and combine with the mustard, water, and grape-seed oil. Transfer to four small sake bowls.

Fourth Tack

Cut the mackerel fillets into bite-sized pieces, spear on toothpicks. Arrange the toothpick spears vertically on a plate. Shake the citrus-soy marinade (Galley Pantry 3) vigorously and pour over the speared fish. Allow to stand for 30 minutes before serving.

Landfall

Use a large chilled plate for the final presentation. Drain the speared mackerel thoroughly and arrange in three rows on each of four plates. Place a small sake bowl of the Celtic mustard on the side of each plate.

Mustard

Galley Pantry 3
Citrus-Soy Marinade
1 clove garlic
1 piece fresh ginger the size of a hazelnut
Juice of 1 orange
Juice of ½ lemon
5 tbs soy sauce
10 tbs grape-seed oil
2 tbs almond oil

Galley Pantry 4
Celtic Marine Mustard
1 tsp cumin seeds
2 sheets Nori (seaweed)
1 tbs Dijon mustard
2 tbs water
4 tbs grape-seed oil

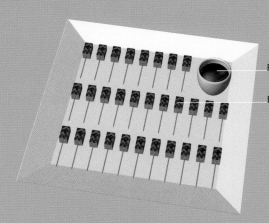

Pot of celtic mustard

Bite-sized mackerel

Setting the Course—When inventing this dish, I looked back to the heroic age of adventure on the Iberian peninsula. The year was 1492. Christopher Columbus was discovering "his" Indies, and Jews and Moors were being forced to emigrate from Spain and Portugal. The geography of the known world was expanding dramatically, and European intellectual assumptions were in a state of flux. This watershed period also witnessed the proliferation of seafaring buccaneers who were vehicles of new ideas, a new political order, new freedoms. This dessert represents more than just carefree sun and sea.

Warm Figs with Spiced Port Wine, Car

Crew of 4

Rigging
Airtight container
Strainer
8 stainless-steel disks measuring ¾ in. (1.5 cm) high
  and 1 in. (2.5 cm) in diameter
Sorbet maker
Coffee mill
4 soup plates
4 saucers
4 small square plates

Cruising Time
12 hours

From the Ship's Hold
Vintage or Late-Bottled Vintage (LBV) Port

Provisions

Galley Pantry 1
Cumin Ice Cream
1 tbs cumin seeds
4 quarts (400 cl) whole milk
6 tbs powdered milk
⅓ cup (100 g) sugar
6 egg yolks
1 tsp bitter-almond extract
⅓ cup (100 g) crème fraîche

Galley Pantry 2
Candied Lemon
1 ½ lemons
¾ cup (175 g) sugar
½ cup (125 g) water

September 10, 2003. Wind from the southwest, force 2 to 3. Calm sea.

First Tack

Cumin ice cream (Galley Pantry 1): Heat a dry frying pan and toast the cumin seeds for a few minutes. Do not allow to color. Cool the seeds and pulverize in the coffee mill. Place the milk, powdered milk, and half the sugar in a large pot and bring to the boil, stirring constantly. Whip the other half of the sugar with the egg yolks for 5 minutes, or until pale. Pour the hot milk-and-sugar mixture onto the egg yolks, return to the pot, and continue cooking as for custard sauce. Add the cumin seeds and steep for 30 minutes. Add the bitter-almond extract. Strain, stir in the crème fraîche, place in a sorbet maker and transfer to freezer.

Second Tack

Candied lemon (Galley Pantry 2): Cut the lemons into thin slices. Make a syrup with the water and sugar. Add the lemon slices and simmer very slowly (approx. 3 hours). When the lemons are cooked, remove from pan and chop.

Third Tack

Ginger florentines (Galley Pantry 3): Combine the crème fraîche, butter, sugar, and honey in a pan. Simmer until the mixture is caramel-colored. Remove pan from heat and add the preserved ginger, flour, and toasted sesame seeds. Mix well. Allow this dough to rest, then press it into the small stainless-steel disks. Fill the disks only up to the three-quarters mark. Preheat the oven to 325°F (170°C). Bake the filled disks for 6 minutes, remove from oven, reverse onto a cake rack, and allow to cool. When cool, carefully remove the Florentines from the metal disks and store in an airtight container.

Fourth Tack

Figs with Port wine (Galley Pantry 4): In a pot, combine the Port wine, all the spices listed, and the honey. Heat to boiling, add the figs, reduce the heat, and simmer for about 15 minutes. Pierce the figs in several places with a wooden toothpick so that they expand and absorb as much of the spice flavor as possible. When the figs are cooked, drain them. Reduce the juice in the pan by one-half.

Landfall

Reheat the figs briefly in the oven. Cut them in half and arrange three halves vertically in each of four soup plates. Garnish each segment with a little candied lemon. Place two of the small ginger Florentines to the right of the figs and top with an oblong of cumin ice cream. Just before serving, reheat the reduced juice that the figs were cooked in. Pour this into the bottom of each plate. Serve.

died Lemon, and Cumin Ice Cream

Galley Pantry 3
Ginger-Sesame Florentines
⅔ cup (150 g) crème fraîche
3 tbs (45 g) butter
2 tbs sugar
1 tsp honey
1 tsp preserved ginger
2 tbs flour
3 tsp toasted sesame seeds

Galley Pantry 4
Figs with Port Wine
12 dark figs
½ bottle Port wine
½ stick cinnamon
2 stars Chinese anise
1 vanilla bean (pod)
2 tbs Ouessant honey

Fig
Candied lemon
Cumin ice cream
Florentine

Chili pepper: The fiery spice
latitude 17°3'0" N, longitude 96°43'0" W

Mexico. The Aztecs and Incas used chili peppers for thousands of years before they became known in the West.

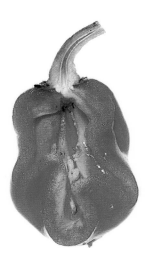

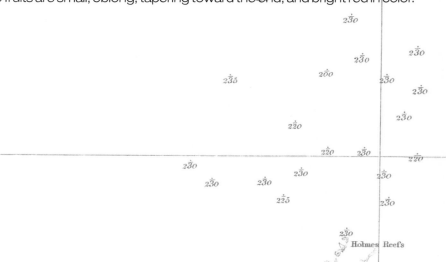

History

The Aztecs and Incas used chili peppers for thousands of years before they became known in the West. Christopher Columbus discovered the long, thin chili peppers when he landed in America, and brought them back to Spain in 1493. The pretty red fruits were initially grown for decoration. From Spain, the plant spread to Greece, Turkey, and on to Hungary. The great Portuguese navigators introduced it to India in the sixteenth century, and from there it spread throughout southeast Asia and China. Chili peppers became such an important ingredient in Indian cooking that many people wrongly believe that they are native to India. One reason why Indian and African cooking relies so heavily on chili peppers is that they are used to counteract the excessively hot climate.

Natural history

Chili peppers are the fruit of the capsicum plant, which is a small shrub belonging to the *Solanaceae* family. There are two main types of peppers. The first is *Capsicum annuum*, better known as capsicums, bell peppers, or sweet peppers, which grow in temperate climates such as Hungary (where it is used in the form of paprika), Bulgaria, Spain, Portugal, and Morocco. The second type is *Capsicum frutescens*, the chili pepper, which grows in hot climates. Around one hundred varieties are known, all very different in shape, size, color, and the intensity of the chili taste. Among the best-known varieties are the African pilipili, Cayenne peppers, jalapeno, pimiento, and hanabero. They are all the fruits of shrubs that grow about three feet (one meter) tall. The fruits are small, oblong, tapering toward the end, and bright red in color.

92

Qualities

Chili peppers are close in taste to pepper. The cultivated varieties range in taste from relatively mild to eye-wateringly fiery, depending on their capsaicin content. The general rule of thumb is the brighter the color, the hotter the chili. While *Capsicum annuum* gives mild red or green peppers with a long-lasting taste, *Capsicum frutescens* is much more intensely fiery. The chili taste tends to have a stimulant effect; the consumer's mouth and the palate feel as if they are on fire.

Uses

Chili peppers have often been used instead of pepper. Their taste is cleaner and more direct. Care should be taken when using chili peppers, as they can easily overpower other ingredients, but they are indispensable for balancing the flavor of some dishes. With the exception of vanilla and cacao, it was the only spice used by the Aztecs to flavor their meat and fish.

How I use chili peppers depends where in the world I am. In the West Indies, I follow the example of the locals and simply rub a Caribbean Scotch bonnet pepper, split down the middle, over bread, fish, or vegetables. In the sweltering heat of Thailand, I drink the local bouillons that are so fiery that the experience is physically painful, and somehow I feel strangely powerful afterwards—and even ask for more. In India, I love the aroma of chili peppers freshly crushed between two rocks, which tickles the nose and makes the eyes water. I love chili peppers crushed together with a few coriander leaves, baby onions, and parsley—to flavor a sauce, for example.

Like pepper, chili peppers are used all over the world. In less than four hundred years, it has become an indispensable ingredient in all sorts of world cuisines. It can be used in such a variety of ways that it is hardly surprising that specialist breeders are trying to come up with ever hotter, fierier varieties.

The finest chili peppers

My favorite chili peppers are Espelette peppers from the Basque country in southwestern France. The best green, yellow, and red peppers are likewise grown in Spain, France, and Italy.

The best Hungarian paprika comes from Szégedin and Kololcza.

Indian cooking uses an almost infinite variety of spice mixes with ground chili peppers. My personal favorite comes from Rajasthan.

Chili peppers are originally native to the Caribbean and Mexico. The best variety here is Cayenne pepper. In Africa, the best chili peppers come from Nigeria, Zanzibar, and Uganda.

Health benefits

Capsaicin, which gives chili peppers their fiery taste, is effective in treating lumbago, neuralgia, and rheumatism. Scientists are currently working on a chili-based painkiller, as it has been demonstrated that capsaicin has a numbing effect on pain receptors. Finally, chili pepper is an age-old remedy against seasickness and drunkenness. It is also high in vitamins A and C.

Setting the Course—The exciting life of a buccaneer forged strong characters. These men were children of La Mancha, raised along the coasts of Spain and Africa and initiated early into the perils of the closely patrolled Mediterranean. Many spent their turbulent teenage years in the Caribbean and then, as adults, sailed to glory on the Indian Ocean or the far-distant Seas of China. If they were lucky, they returned in old age—rich and famous at last—to the safe haven of Saint-Malo. The men who lived such lives developed habits to sustain them through their hardships, and they adapted their tastes to new experiences. By necessity, of course; but also, sometimes, by inclination—for the sheer pleasure of it. To help them bear the absence of faraway loved ones, they enlivened their daily fare with that "opium of the gourmet," chili pepper. Chili pepper traveled everywhere with wandering adventurers, conditioning their taste buds and leaving an indelible mark on their memories.

Spider Crab with Buccaneer's Triple

94

Crew of 4

Rigging
12 stainless-steel disks, 1 ½ in.
   (4 cm) high, 1 ¼ in. (3 cm) in
   diameter
Small handheld blender

Cruising Time
2 hours

From the Ship's Hold
Crozes-Hermitage Blanc

Provisions

Galley Pantry 1
4 spider crabs weighing about 2 lb.
   (1 kg) each, preferably 2 females
   + 2 males (the males are easier to
   shell, the females often contain
   more coral)
10 quarts water + ⅔ cup (200 g)
   coarse salt + 1 tsp Cayenne
   pepper
4 sprigs parsley
4 slices yeast bread
2 fresh Caribbean chili peppers,
   each halved

Galley Pantry 2
Coraline Seasoning
(see page 71)

Galley Pantry 3
Oriental Seasoning
Vinaigrette
1 tbs rice vinegar
½ cup (10 cl) grape-seed oil
1 pinch sugar
¼ cup (5 cl) soy sauce

May 7, 2000. Chilly wind from the northwest, force 5. Cloudy skies, clearing in patches.

First Tack

Cook the spider crabs in 10 quarts boiling water with the coarse salt and Cayenne pepper, counting 20 minutes after second boil. Remove crabs from pot and cool. Cut off the heads and tails, scoop out the coral, and set aside. Shell the bodies and claws, set the crabmeat aside.

Second Tack

Add 4 tbs coral to the ingredients for the vinaigrette listed on page 71, place in jar, close tightly, and shake to blend. Combine the ingredients for the vinaigrette listed under Galley Pantry 3, place in jar, close tightly, and shake to blend. Combine the ingredients for the vinaigrette listed under Galley Pantry 4, place in jar, close tightly, and shake to blend. For the rougail (Galley Pantry 3, peel and dice the carrots, onions, garlic clove, and ginger. Add the juice of ½ lime, the muscovado sugar, olive oil, salt, and chili pepper paste. Grate ½ of the mango into this mixture and stir to combine.

Third Tack

Divide the crabmeat into three equal portions. To the first third, add the remaining coral and the chopped parsley leaves (Galley Pantry 1). Set aside 4 tbs of the vinaigrette from Galley Pantry 2 and stir the rest gently into the crab-and-coral mixture. Use this mixture to fill four of the disks. Refrigerate the filled disks. For the second third of the crabmeat, proceed as for the first, adding half of the rougail mixture and the chopped coriander leaves. Set aside 4 tbs of the vinaigrette from Galley Pantry 3 and add the remainder to the crabmeat mixture. Fill four more disks and refrigerate. For the final third of the crabmeat, proceed as for the first two, adding the chopped basil leaves. Set aside 4 tbs of the vinaigrette from Galley Pantry 4 and add the remainder to the crabmeat mixture. Fill the final four disks with this mixture and refrigerate.

Landfall

Toast the slices of bread and cut each slice into three rectangles. Place three of the disks, one for each separate crabmeat mixture, on a large plate. Repeat until all four plates are filled. Remove the disks, pressing lightly on the crabmeat with the index finger and sliding the disks upwards. Pour a thin stream of the remaining vinaigrette onto the mounds of crabmeat, using a different vinaigrette for each separate mound. Place three toast rectangles on the edge of each plate and garnish with ½ a small Caribbean chili pepper (Galley Pantry 1). This "fiery" ingredient can be rubbed on the bread and/or the crabmeat for an extra touch of spicy intensity.

Spice

Rougail
¼ cup (50 g) baby carrots
¼ cup (50 g) baby onions
½ clove garlic
1 knob fresh ginger
½ lime
1 tsp muscovado sugar
¼ cup (5 cl) olive oil
1 dash Thai chili pepper paste
Salt
1 small green mango
6 coriander leaves

Galley Pantry 4
Moorish Seasoning
½ clove garlic
1 preserved chili pepper (peeled, seeded pimiento)
2 black peppercorns
1 lime
½ cup (10 cl) olive oil
1 pinch powdered Espelette chili pepper
3 leaves basil

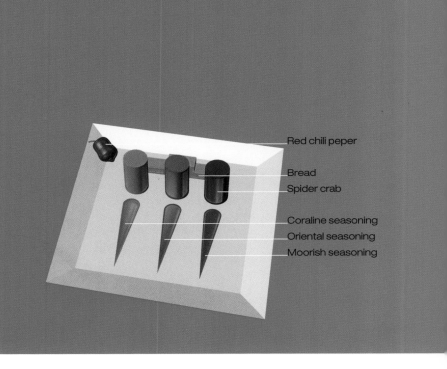

Red chili peper

Bread

Spider crab

Coraline seasoning

Oriental seasoning

Moorish seasoning

Setting the Course—During the heroic era of seafaring adventurers, providing food on board was always a huge problem. In a number of works dealing with the maritime exploits of the seventeenth and eighteenth centuries, I've found accounts describing the invention of a blend of spices intended to improve the often dubious taste of certain ships' stores. This blend was composed of ground chili pepper, thyme, mustard seeds, cumin seeds, and stale bread. The powder was apparently a staple on all Spanish, Portuguese, British, Dutch, and French vessels. In the course of my research, I've never found exact proportions for this mixture. I therefore invented my own recipe for it, dubbing my powder "Nevis" after the small Caribbean island. I like to picture those Old-World fleets, combing the tiny islands of the Caribbean in search of the legendary mermaid known as the "Beauty of Tongking."

Nevis Scallops, Tongking Bean Emu

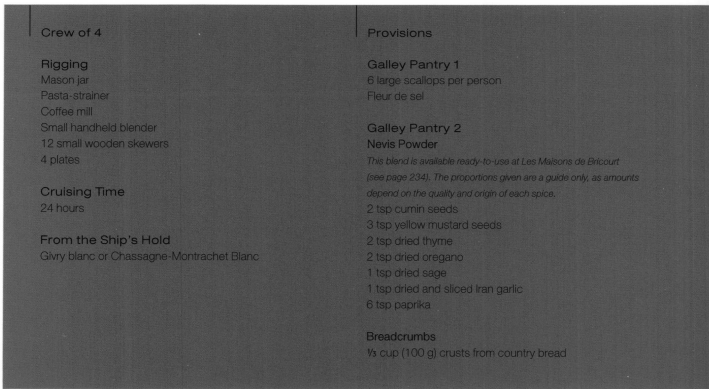

Crew of 4

Rigging
Mason jar
Pasta-strainer
Coffee mill
Small handheld blender
12 small wooden skewers
4 plates

Cruising Time
24 hours

From the Ship's Hold
Givry blanc or Chassagne-Montrachet Blanc

Provisions

Galley Pantry 1
6 large scallops per person
Fleur de sel

Galley Pantry 2
Nevis Powder
This blend is available ready-to-use at Les Maisons de Bricourt
(see page 234). The proportions given are a guide only, as amounts
depend on the quality and origin of each spice.
2 tsp cumin seeds
3 tsp yellow mustard seeds
2 tsp dried thyme
2 tsp dried oregano
1 tsp dried sage
1 tsp dried and sliced Iran garlic
6 tsp paprika

Breadcrumbs
⅓ cup (100 g) crusts from country bread

October 2000. Wind from the southwest, force 1. Blue skies . . . Indian Summer.

First Tack

The night before, prepare the Nevis breadcrumbs (Galley Pantry 2). Crumble the crusts of country bread and combine with all the spices except for the paprika. Dry out this mixture for 2½ hours in an oven heated to 212°F (100°C). Set aside in a dry place until the next day. Prepare the Tongking emulsion (Galley Pantry 3). In the Mason jar, combine the grape-seed oil and chopped Tonka bean. Close the jar tightly and sterilize, counting 5 minutes after second boil. Allow to stand in the water bath until the next day.

Second Tack

The next day, finish the Nevis breadcrumbs (Galley Pantry 2). Grind the bread and spices briefly in a coffee mill. The breadcrumbs should remain somewhat coarse. Sift the crumbs through a pasta-strainer. Add the paprika to the crumbs and store in an airtight container. The crumbs will keep well. Remove the scallops (Galley Pantry 1) from their shells, rinse well, and dry thoroughly. Set aside in a strainer. Leek garnish (Galley Pantry 4): Trim off the outer green leaves of the leeks, cut the white stalks in four lengthwise. Rinse well and chop. Cook in a large pot of boiling salted water for 3 minutes after second boil. Drain and refresh in ice water. Drain again and transfer to a pot with the olive oil, salt, and pepper.

Third Tack

A few hours before serving, prepare the Tongking emulsion (Galley Pantry 3). Set aside the 3 tbs chicken bouillon for finishing the emulsion. Combine the remaining ingredients in an ample receptacle such as a large (2-cup) measuring cup, and blend with the handheld blender, gradually incorporating the strained Tongking oil. Prepare a double-boiler for reheating the emulsion. Prepare the Nevis scallops (Galley Pantry 1 + Galley Pantry 2). Sauté the scallops on one side only in a nonstick frying pan. Thread the scallops in pairs on the small wooden skewers, cooked side out. Dredge the skewers in the Nevis breadcrumbs and arrange vertically in the baking dish.

Landfall

Final cooking. Preheat oven to 350°F (180°C). Heat the water in the double-boiler to a simmer. Bake the scallops, which should remain in a vertical position supported by each other, for 6 to 8 minutes. Meanwhile, heat the emulsion in the top of the double-boiler, whipping with a wire whisk until thick. Remove from double-boiler and add the 3 remaining tbs chicken bouillon. Adjust the seasoning. Rapidly reheat the leek garnish. Arrange a row of the leek garnish down a line marking the first third on each of four warm serving plates. Pour a line of the Tongking emulsion on either side of the leeks. Remove the scallops from the skewers and arrange on the remaining two-thirds of the plates. Finish by dribbling a few drops of olive oil and a little fleur de sel over the scallops.

sion

Galley Pantry 3
Tongking Emulsion
¾ cup (20 cl) grape-seed oil
1 small Tonka bean
5 tbs chicken bouillon + 3 tbs for finishing the emulsion
1 tbs Chardonnay white-wine vinegar
1 egg white

Galley Pantry 4
Garnish
4 very tender medium leeks
2 tbs quality olive oil
Salt and freshly-ground pepper

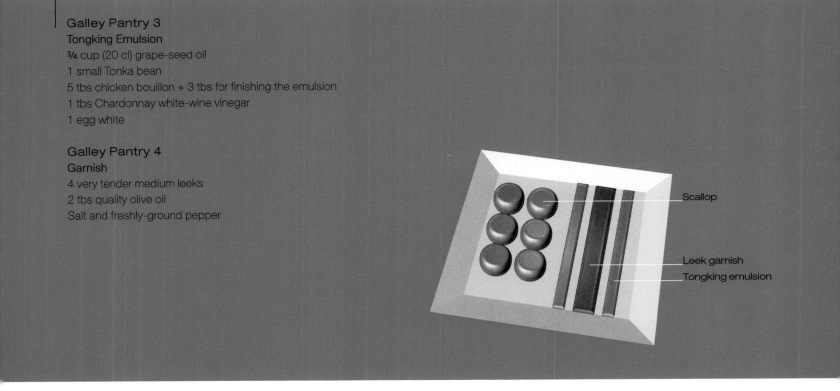

Scallop

Leek garnish
Tongking emulsion

Setting the Course—I would be tempted to agree with those who claim the only "intelligent" cuisine is the bitter kind. This is because ways must be found to tame its aggressive character. Sweet cuisine, on the other hand, is almost too easy. But everyone agrees on the dual appeal of sweet, almost sugary angelica contrasted with a bitter, biting backdrop of chili pepper. Here we come near to perfection. The earthy flavor of the deceptively demure angelica is absolutely stunning, especially when it plays with fire . . . the fire of chili pepper. Fresh goat cheese from verdant pastures calms the storm and leaves an impression of lightness and harmony—like the peaceful calm of a warm summer's nightfall.

Fresh Goat Cheese, Bell Peppers,

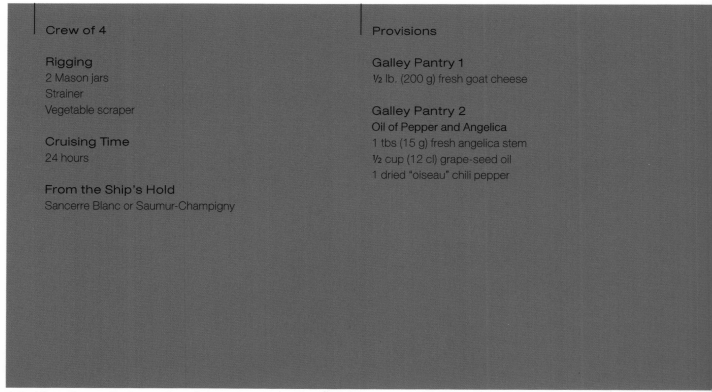

Crew of 4

Rigging
2 Mason jars
Strainer
Vegetable scraper

Cruising Time
24 hours

From the Ship's Hold
Sancerre Blanc or Saumur-Champigny

Provisions

Galley Pantry 1
½ lb. (200 g) fresh goat cheese

Galley Pantry 2
Oil of Pepper and Angelica
1 tbs (15 g) fresh angelica stem
½ cup (12 cl) grape-seed oil
1 dried "oiseau" chili pepper

August 7, 2003. Wind from the north, force 2 to 3. Calm seas; some cloud cover.

First Tack

Oil of angelica and pepper (Galley Pantry 2): Rinse and dry the fresh angelica stem, dice, and place in a Mason jar with the grape-seed oil. Remove the seeds (if you're afraid of "fire") from the "oiseau" chili pepper and add the pepper to the contents of the jar. Close jar tightly and sterilize in a water bath, counting 10 minutes after second boil. Cool in the water bath overnight.

Second Tack

Preserved bell peppers (Galley Pantry 3): Cut the two bell pepper halves into strips ¾ in. (2 cm) wide. Cut out the white membrane, remove the seeds. Using a vegetable scraper, peel the skin off each strip. Chop the skinned strips. Place the chopped peppers in another Mason jar with the olive and sunflower oils. Close jar tightly and sterilize in a water bath for 10 minutes after second boil. Remove jar from the water bath and cool at room temperature. Refrigerate when cool.

Third Tack

A few hours before serving, prepare the herbs (Galley Pantry 4). Rinse the bunches of purslane and wood sorrel. Set aside. Combine the Espelette pepper with the fleur de sel, set aside. Cut the fresh goat cheese into 16 sticks and arrange in two rows on each of four plates. Set aside.

Landfall

Drain the preserved bell peppers. Strain the oil of angelica and pepper. Add one-half of this oil to the bell peppers. Arrange the peppers in oil on serving plates between two rows of goat-cheese sticks. Garnish the tip of each goat-cheese stick with a leaf of wood sorrel. Sprinkle all these ingredients with fleur de sel and Espelette pepper. Serve.

Chili Pepper, and Angelica Oil

Galley Pantry 3
Preserved Bell Peppers (will keep for several weeks)
½ red bell pepper
½ yellow bell pepper
6 tbs sunflower oil
3 tbs olive oil

Galley Pantry 4
The Herbs
4 bunches purslane
16 leaves wood sorrel
Finishing
1 tsp fleur de sel
1 tsp Espelette pepper

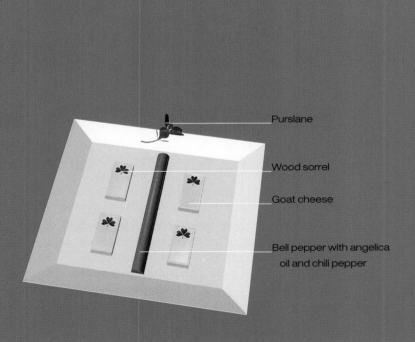

Purslane

Wood sorrel

Goat cheese

Bell pepper with angelica oil and chili pepper

Star anise:
The Fragrant star
latitude 31°4'10" N, longitude 121°15'56" E

China. Star anise originated in the Yunnan region of China. It crossed the Himalayas and became an indispensable ingredient in Indian cooking.

History

Star anise originated in the Yunnan region of China. It crossed the Himalayas and became an indispensable ingredient in Indian cooking. It is recorded as having reached Russia in the Middle Ages, but was still unknown in Europe at that time. Star anise reached Europe—London, to be precise—in 1588, when the British navigator Thomas Cavendish returned from sailing around the world. He discovered the spice when he stopped off in the Philippines. The new spice was much admired, particularly by a certain Morgan, apothecary to Queen Elizabeth I. He sent samples of the spice to a number of leading European apothecaries. The highly perfumed stars were soon widely used in jams and liqueurs. The port of Bordeaux specialized in the star anise trade: local merchants invented a liqueur called anisette which is still used today as the basis for a number of popular and refreshing aniseed-flavored aperitifs.

Natural history

Star anise is the fruit of *Illicium verum*, a beautiful tree that is a member of the *Magnoliaceae* family. The spice takes its name from the shape of the individual fruits, which are eight-pointed stars. The fruits are picked before they ripen and then dried in the sun. The yellow fruit turns blue, then brown. The tree itself smells strongly of aniseed.

Qualities

Although star anise does not come from the same *Umbellifera* family as anise and fennel, it does have a very similar sweet licorice taste. Star anise has a little more bite than aniseed. The seeds are less flavorsome than the fruit.

Uses

Star anise has always been a feature of Chinese cuisine. It is one of the spices in the famous five-spice mix, along with Szechuan pepper, cinnamon, fennel, and cloves. It is also widely used in Indian curries.

It was very popular in seventeenth-century Europe, but has since fallen largely out of favor there, except as an ingredient of aniseed aperitifs. Recently, it has made something of a comeback in ready-mixed Five Spices preparations for oven-cooked fish. I always add a few pieces of star anise to my nage sauces and fish stocks.

The finest star anise

The very best star anise is grown in the region of Lang Son, in Tonkin in northern Vietnam.

If you are ever in Japan, you should be aware that a very similar-looking plant called *Illicus religiosum* is often found in Japanese cemeteries. Take care not to confuse the two, as *Illicus religiosum* is poisonous.

Health benefits

Star anise is good for digestion. At the end of a heavy meal, Indians eat a few pinches of pan, which is a mix of seeds including star anise. Star anise both stimulates the appetite and aids digestion—perfect for gourmets!

Setting the Course—This dish boasts an intriguing combination of highly contrasting flavors and textures. To tie together the slight sweetness of the lamb's lettuce, elasticity of the squid, and somewhat bitter suavity of the golden foie gras, I confected a clear, crisp bouillon. Accented with the star anise, the bouillon plays a role similar to that of a crisp breeze on a spring morning. The rosemary is also unexpected, but it contributes to the overall balance of the dish.

Foie Gras, Squid, Fennel Apple, and

Crew of 4

Rigging
Coffee mill
2 nonstick frying pans
Mason jar
Strainer
Small handheld blender
4 soup plates

Cruising Time
24 hours

From the Ship's Hold
Côteaux du Languedoc Blanc

Provisions

Galley Pantry 1
1 ½ lb. (700 g) small whole squid
1 lb. (500 g) raw foie gras; the quality and freshness of the foie gras will have a decisive impact on the final result
1 tbs olive oil
Salt, freshly-ground pepper

Galley Pantry 2
Mixed Spices
1 star anise
1 tbs green anise seeds
1 tbs fennel seeds
3 tbs cumin seeds
1 tbs coriander seeds
Rosemary Powder
½ bunch fresh rosemary
1 tsp salt
½ tsp sugar

May 3, 2001. Lilacs in bloom. Wind from the southwest, force 4 to 5. Cloudy skies; rough seas.

First Tack

The night before, prepare the rosemary powder (Galley Pantry 2). Preheat oven to 175°F (80°C). Place the rosemary in the oven and dry out until it breaks easily. Cool, and then grind in the coffee mill with the salt and sugar (Galley Pantry 2). Place in airtight container and set aside. Place the spices (Galley Pantry 2) in the coffee mill and pulverize. Transfer to another airtight container and set aside. Preparing the Chinese-anise oil (Galley Pantry 4). Crush the Chinese anise with the blender, place in the Mason jar, add the grape-seed oil. Close the jar tightly and sterilize in a water bath, counting 10 minutes from second boil. Cool overnight. Strain before using.

Second Tack

A few hours before serving, prepare the squid (Galley Pantry 1). Remove the heads, interior cartilage, and all scraps of skin. Rinse well and slice into rounds. Set aside in a drainer. Separate the two lobes of the foie gras and cut each one into four equal cubic pieces. Refrigerate.

Third Tack

Preparing the garnish (Galley Pantry 3): Chop the ¼ Chinese cabbage into small, even pieces. Peel the red onion and cut into thin slices. Remove leaves from the fennel apple and chop. Combine all these ingredients and refrigerate.

Landfall

Preheat oven to 350°F (180°C). Season the portions of foie gras with salt and freshly-ground pepper, then sauté on both sides in a nonstick frying pan. Transfer to a plate covered with absorbent paper and set aside at room temperature. Scrape up the juices in the pan and add the juice of two lemons, the vegetable bouillon (Galley Pantry 4), and 1 tsp mixed spices (Galley Pantry 2). Reduce by one-third. Strain and keep hot. Transfer the absorbent paper with the foie gras on it to the oven and bake for 6 to 8 minutes. Meanwhile, take two frying pans: quickly sauté the rounds of squid in 1 tbs olive oil in one, and sauté the Chinese cabbage mixture in 1 tbs olive oil in another. Season the squid with the rosemary powder. Sprinkle the squid and cabbage with salt and pepper. In warm soup plates, arrange a mound of cabbage, onion, and fennel apple. Place two cubes of foie gras on one side of each plate, and the rounds of squid on the other. Pour some of the acidulated bouillon into each plate and dot with drops of the Chinese-anise oil. Serve.

Rosemary

Galley Pantry 3
Garnish
¼ Chinese cabbage
1 small red onion
A few sprigs fennel apple
1 tbs olive oil

Galley Pantry 4
Tangy Bouillon
2 lemons
2 cups (½ liter) vegetable bouillon
Chinese-Anise Oil
4 Chinese-anise stars
½ cup (12 cl) grape-seed oil

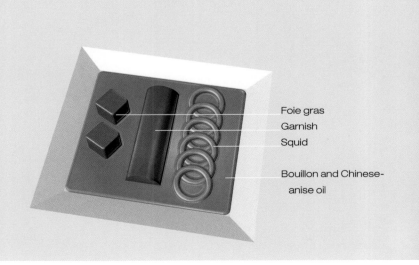

Foie gras
Garnish
Squid

Bouillon and Chinese-anise oil

Setting the Course—For generations my family has relished fillets of solette (baby sole), lightly browned in salted butter. We also love this fish's crunchy barbels, which we always save. What's different about this recipe? The new potatoes, of course, and also the subtle hints of anise and the distinctive flavor afforded by the seaweed.

Golden Baby Sole and Mashed Pota

Crew of 4

Rigging
Mason jar
Coffee mill
Nonstick frying pan
Strainer
4 plates

Cruising Time
24 hours

From the Ship's Hold
Chablis Premier Cru

Provisions

Galley Pantry 1
8 whole baby soles weighing 8–12 oz. (250–300 g) each
2 tbs (25 g) salted butter

The Sauce
2 tbs (25 g) salted butter
1 tbs sunflower oil
1 tbs "Neptune" powder (see page 111)
3 lemons
1 cup (25 cl) chicken bouillon

June 30, 2000. Northwest wind, force 3 to 4. Frequent showers.

First Tack (to prepare the night before)

The "Neptune" powder (Galley Pantry 2): Toast the sesame seeds in a dry frying pan, allow to cool, and combine with the other spices. Pulverize all the spices in a coffee mill and set aside. Chinese-anise oil (Galley Pantry 3): Place the grape-seed oil and the three Chinese-anise stars in a Mason jar and sterilize in a water bath, counting 10 minutes after second boil. Cool in the water bath until the next day, strain.

Second Tack

First prepare the baby soles (Galley Pantry 1). Slice small incisions near the gills of the fish and use a pair of kitchen shears to cut off the heads, leaving the barbels and tails in place.

Third Tack

One hour before serving, boil the potatoes in salted water (Galley Pantry 4). Peel the cooked potatoes and mash with a fork. Combine with the 3 tbs (40 g) salted butter (Galley Pantry 4). Keep warm. Pre-cooking the baby sole (Galley Pantry 1). Add 2 tbs (25 g) salted butter to a nonstick frying pan. Sauté the fish on both sides until golden. Remove the crisp barbells and tails from the fish and set aside. Arrange the fish in a dish for later reheating.

Fourth Tack

Sauce (Galley Pantry 1): Heat 1 tbs sunflower oil and 2 tbs (25 g) salted butter in a small pan and sauté the barbells and tails of the sole, stirring constantly until golden. Add 1 tbs "Neptune" powder and the juice of the 3 lemons. Scrape well to deglaze the pan, and boil the pan juices until reduced by one-half. Add the chicken bouillon and reduce until the liquid in the pan barely covers the bones. Strain, pressing in order to extract the maximum amount of liquid. Keep warm.

Landfall

Reheat the baby sole for about 5 minutes in a hot oven. Reheat the sauce. Check the mashed potatoes and reheat if necessary. Pour two parallel lines of Chinese-Anise oil and "Neptune" powder onto the serving plates, and arrange the baby soles in the center. Place a tablespoon of the mashed potato in the corner opposite the oil and powder, garnish with the chopped fennel apple. Pour the sauce over the fish. Serve.

es with Anise Flavorings from Near and Far

Galley Pantry 2
"Neptune" Powder

This mixture is available ready-to-use from Les Maisons de Bricourt (see page 234). The proportions given are a guide only, since amounts depend on the quality and origin of each spice.

1 tsp sesame seeds
4 tbs fennel seeds
1 tsp dill
1 Chinese-anise star
1 tsp coriander seeds
1 tbs wakamé (dried seaweed)

Galley Pantry 3
Chinese-Anise Oil

½ cup (12 cl) grape-seed oil
3 Chinese-anise stars

Galley Pantry 4

20 small new potatoes
3 tbs (40 g) salted butter
1 sprig fennel apple

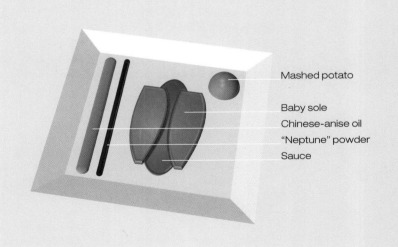

Mashed potato

Baby sole
Chinese-anise oil
"Neptune" powder
Sauce

Setting the Course—On one chilly morning in early winter, I paid a call on the Robin family, "my" vegetable dealers. While we chatted in their warehouse crammed with freshly picked vegetables, they suggested that I sample a warm beet, just out of the pot after six hours of cooking. I found myself overcome by a strong and rare feeling: it inspired me to invent a dessert in which the hint of organic iodine that is characteristic of this vegetable is combined with Yuletide citrus and Chinese anise. My crowning touch is a dollop of smooth farmhouse cream.

Beets with Warm Chinese-Anise Syrup

Crew of 4

Rigging
Strainer
Small handheld blender
Sorbet maker
4 plates

Cruising Time
24 hours

From the Ship's Hold
Gewürztraminer

Provisions

Galley Pantry 1
4 freshly cooked beets
1 cup (25 cl) water
⅓ cup (100 g) light brown sugar
½ vanilla bean (pod)
2 Chinese-anise stars

Galley Pantry 2
Tangerine-and-Pomegranate Marmalade
6 + 1 tangerines
2 tbs (25 g) sugar
¾ cup (20 cl) water
2 pomegranates
½ cup (10 cl) heavy cream
1 scant tbs (10 g) sugar

November 4, 2004. Wind from the North, force 3 to 4. Rough seas, stormy sky.

First Tack
Peel the beets (Galley Pantry 1), cut into 1-inch (2-cm) cubes. Place the water, sugar, Chinese anise, and vanilla in a pot. Bring to a boil and reduce to one-fourth original volume. Steep the cubed beets in this syrup for 4 hours. Leave the beets in one-half of the syrup and reduce the remainder to one-third its original volume.

Second Tack
Tangerine-and-pomegranate marmalade (Galley Pantry 2): Wash the fruit. Cut the six tangerines into thin slices and remove the seeds. Add the sugar, stir. Refrigerate this mixture and allow to steep for 12 hours. At the end of the steeping period, add the water to the tangerines and sugar, bring to a boil, and simmer for one hour, stirring often. At the last moment, add the seeds of the two pomegranates. Cool and refrigerate.

Third Tack
Lemon sorbet (Galley Pantry 3): Prepare a syrup with the sugar, water, and Chinese-anise stars (Galley Pantry 3). Bring to a boil and simmer for 2 minutes. Cool the syrup, then add the lemon juice and lightly beaten egg white. Blend this mixture thoroughly, transfer to sorbet maker, and store in freezer.

Landfall
Whip the cream with the 1 tbs (10 g) sugar (Galley Pantry 2). Fold the sweetened whipped cream lightly into the tangerine marmalade. Warm the cubed beets in the reduced beet syrup. Arrange 3 warm beet cubes on each serving plate. Garnish with a generous ribbon of the creamy marmalade, cover with beet syrup. Grate the rind of the remaining tangerine (Galley Pantry 2) over everything on the plate. Add a spoonful of the Chinese-anise flavored lemon sorbet on the side. Serve.

Tangerine-and-Pomegranate Marmalade

Galley Pantry 3
Chinese-Anise Flavored Lemon Sorbet
1 generous cup (30 cl) water
½ cup (120 g) sugar
4 Chinese-anise stars
1 cup (25 cl) lemon juice
1 egg white

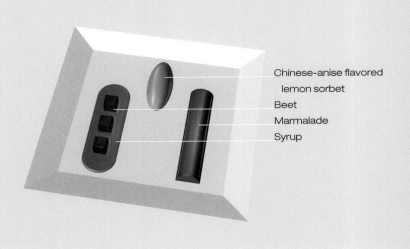

Chinese-anise flavored lemon sorbet
Beet
Marmalade
Syrup

Tomatoes: Tart and juicy
latitude: 15°34'95" S, longitude 74°2'47" W

Peru. The Peruvian Incas grew a small type of tomato—rather like our cherry tomatoes—for centuries before they were discovered by the Europeans.

History

The Peruvian Incas grew a small type of tomato—rather like our cherry tomatoes—for centuries before they were discovered by the Europeans. The first tomato plantation in Europe was in Seville in Spain, where tomatoes were grown by monks. From there, tomatoes quickly spread to the rest of Spain, southern France, and Italy, where the peasants were delighted by this new food source. However, the European courts distrusted tomatoes. In the sixteenth century, the Italian aristocracy considered tomatoes to be a powerful aphrodisiac, like mandrake, giving them the magical and evocative name of "love apples." The British were even more distrustful, classifying tomatoes among the deadly poisons to be avoided at all costs, even in the form of medicine.

It was not until the eighteenth century that tomatoes made their first timid appearance in recipes. It had taken the upper ranks of society two and a half centuries to realize what the peasants had always known.

The great tomato-based recipes, the sauces and ratatouilles that are the bedrock of Mediterranean cuisine, all date from the nineteenth century. Settlers took tomatoes with them when they moved to the colonies, which is how tomatoes were introduced to the Middle East and North Africa, where the plants quickly spread.

European immigrants also took tomato plants with them to North America, where the same distrust of the juicy red fruit prevailed until the early twentieth century. For the puritans, tomatoes represented sin, and many believed that eating raw tomatoes would make them very ill. But then ketchup was invented, and America has never looked back.

Tomatoes reached North America by a very roundabout route, from Peru via the Mediterranean basin, then Britain, then finally the United States. Today, tomatoes are used in every major world cuisine.

Natural history

Tomatoes are the fruit of a herbaceous plant from the *Solanaceae* family. They come in a huge variety of shapes, sizes, and colors. Although tomatoes are generally eaten as a vegetable, in botanical terms they are in fact a fruit.

Qualities

The tastiest tomatoes are those fresh picked late on a July morning, when the sun has had time to warm the skin but the heart is still cool and refreshing. Cup the fresh tomato in your palm, close your eyes and inhale its aroma, then bite into the juicy pulp. The taste is smooth and intense, very slightly acid. The flesh is pulpy and inviting.

The tomatoes that are on sale all year round are in general brightly colored but the taste is watery and insipid. The taste of hothouse tomatoes as we know them today is very different from the taste of wild tomatoes from Peru. Unfortunately, the multinational food companies prefer varieties that give a good yield over those that have a rich taste. The result is that the flavor has been bred out of many best-selling varieties. However, the news is not all bad: in recent years, plant breeders have been reversing the trend, returning to more old-fashioned, highly flavored tomatoes.

Uses

I love the way my wife, Jane, uses raw tomatoes in salads. She removes the skin by taking off the stalk, cutting a small cross through the skin on the bottom, and dipping the tomato in boiling water for a few seconds before plunging it into cold water and removing the skin. She then cuts the tomato into four or six parts, removes the pips, and dribbles them with a vinaigrette made of one soup spoon of sherry vinegar, two soup spoons of olive oil, two soup spoons of sunflower oil, a pinch of sugar, a pinch of salt, a twist of pepper, and a dash of Espelette chili pepper.

Leave the tomatoes to marinate in the vinaigrette for an hour before serving. Scatter a few fresh herbs over them—whatever you happen to have to hand—and serve them at room temperature. Keep the leftover sauce for another salad or for brushing over steam-cooked fish.

The finest tomatoes

It is almost impossible to choose between the two thousand or so varieties available. The best tomatoes are the ones that grow in your own garden, fresh picked for use. There is nothing easier than growing a few tomato plants in a sunny corner of the garden or even on a balcony. My favorites depend on which recipe I have in mind:

- Oxheart tomatoes for stuffing
- The pink Rose de Berne for salads
- Firm, tasty Marmandes for oven-cooking whole
- Tomatoes from the Andes for candying
- Immaculate white tomatoes from Quebec for their stunning aesthetic effect
- The Priscas from my own garden for my homemade chutneys

Health benefits

Tomatoes are very rich in energy and antioxidants and are excellent for the liver. They also help fight high blood pressure. They can be used to treat sunburn and are often used in cosmetics to combat oily skin.

Setting the Course—It's strange, but I find strolling down a row of tomato plants in midsummer absolutely intoxicating. My next thought is inevitably how I might use fish as the basis for weaving all these tomatoes into a compelling story. I have long dreamed of inventing a composition fit for a sort of Dionysus of the seas—Neptune's brother. In this recipe the tomato—true to its generous Mediterranean nature—enhances the fish with its depth, its refreshing contrast of sweet-and-sour, its mellowness . . . and much more.

Brill with Spiced Tomatoes

Crew of 4	Provisions
Rigging	**Galley Pantry 1**
Large roasting pan	1 brill weighing 4 lbs. (2 kg), skinned and filleted by your
Strainer	fish seller
Small handheld blender	
Aluminum foil	**Galley Pantry 2**
4 soup plates	**Tomato Vinaigrette**
	4 large, very ripe tomatoes
Cruising Time	4 tbs sunflower oil
4 hours	2 tbs sherry vinegar
	2 tbs olive oil
From the Ship's Hold	1 pinch dried oregano
Bandol Rosé	Dash sugar
	½ tsp salt
	1 sprig fresh coriander

August 9, 2003. Calm seas, gentle evening breezes.

First Tack

Tomato garnish (Galley Pantry 3): For the sweet-sour crushed tomatoes: Plunge the tomatoes into boiling water for a few moments, drain, peel, cut in half and remove the seeds. Chop the tomatoes. Peel the garlic clove, chop the new onion. Place the onion in a pot with the olive oil and sauté briefly. Add the chopped tomatoes, garlic clove, pinch of dried oregano, granulated sugar, and cider vinegar. Simmer this mixture until all the liquid has been absorbed. Set aside in the pot. For the cherry tomato preserves: plunge the tomatoes into boiling water for a few moments and peel without removing the stems. Sprinkle lightly with salt and sugar and allow to rest for 30 minutes. Transfer the tomatoes to a pot and add enough of the olive and basil oils to cover them almost completely. Set aside at room temperature. For the semi-cooked tomatoes: Slice the yellow tomatoes without peeling. Roll the slices in olive oil, sprinkle with salt and pepper. Place in a baking dish and set aside. Remove the dried tomatoes from oil, drain well, and add to the baking dish with the yellow tomatoes.

Second Tack

Tomato vinaigrette (Galley Pantry 2): In a bowl combine the sunflower oil, sherry vinegar, olive oil, dried oregano, sugar, salt, sprig of coriander, and the four large whole tomatoes. Blend thoroughly with handheld blender. Strain, pressing the pulp well in order to extract as much pulp as possible. Set aside.

Third Tack

The brill (Galley Pantry 1): Cut the fish fillets into 12 even rectangles. Spread them in a baking dish, smoothing them so they will lie flat. They should not overlap. Pour enough vinaigrette over the fillets to barely cover. Place the remaining vinaigrette in a pot ready for reheating later. Seal the baking dish with a sheet of aluminum foil. Preheat oven to 300°F (150°C).

Landfall

Bake the fish for 6 minutes. Slip the dish of yellow and dried tomatoes into the oven with the fish just long enough to reheat. Reheat the sweet-sour crushed tomatoes without boiling. Place 1 tbs of the sweet-sour crushed tomatoes in each of four soup plates. Add three portions of fish and garnish with the other tomato preparations on the side. Pour the vinaigrette around the fish. Add the sprigs of coriander and basil and the borage blossoms. Dot these ingredients with 1 tsp olive oil and top with 1 tsp heavy crème fraîche. Serve.

Galley Pantry 3
Garnish:
Cherry Tomato Preserves (oil)
12 small cherry tomatoes
Salt and sugar
1 cup (25 cl) olive oil
½ cup (12 cl) basil oil
Sweet-Sour Crushed Tomatoes
8 large, very ripe tomatoes
1 clove garlic
1 new onion
1 tbs olive oil
1 pinch dried oregano
1 tbs granulated sugar
3 tbs cider vinegar
Semi-Cooked Tomatoes
6 small, yellow, pear-shaped tomatoes
2 tbs olive oil
Salt and pepper
Dried Tomatoes
12 quarters dried tomatoes (from an Italian grocery)

Galley Pantry 4
Finishing
4 tsp olive oil
4 tsp heavy crème fraîche
2 sprigs small-leaved green basil
12 large coriander leaves
4 borage blossoms

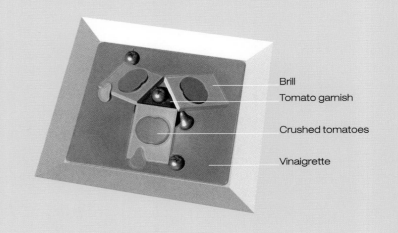

Brill
Tomato garnish
Crushed tomatoes
Vinaigrette

Setting the Course—The tomato presents a paradox. For centuries it was suspected of being poisonous, but now—mixed with vinegar, sugar, and a few spices—it's the basis for one of the most widely consumed condiments in the world: ketchup. My own tomato chutney, which I created to accompany crisp fritters of squid from the bay, also plays on this classic contrast between salt and sweet. Mellow sweetness and tangy bite are combined in this blend of tomatoes and spices in which to dip rounds of the silvery seafood . . . and, once you start eating them, you won't be able to stop!

Fried Squid with "Bricourt" Tomato

Crew of 4

Rigging
Deep-fat fryer or large pot of oil
Coffee mill
4 small ramekins
4 plates

Cruising Time
12 hours

From the Ship's Hold
Champagne Brut

Provisions

Galley Pantry 1
4 squid weighing ½ lb. (200 g) each

Galley Pantry 2
Fritter Batter
⅓ cup (100 g) flour
⅓ cup (100 g) potato flour
2 tsp (10 g) baking powder
1 dash Espelette pepper
¾ cup (20 cl) lager

July 2, 2000. Wind from the northwest, force 3 to 4. Gentle, warm late-evening breeze.

First Tack

Mixed spices (Galley Pantry 4): Pulverize the cardamom, mace, and cloves in a coffee mill. Add the paprika and sugar, then grind again briefly. Set aside. The tomato chutney (Galley Pantry 3) should be prepared at least six hours in advance. First, plunge the tomatoes for a few moments in boiling water, then drain, peel, seed, and chop them. Chop the onion and garlic. Cooking the chutney is a two-step process. First, sauté the onion with the 2 tbs olive oil. Do not allow to color. Add the garlic, tomatoes, and mixed ground spices. Add the sugar and one-half of the cider vinegar. Simmer until all the liquid has evaporated. Add the remaining vinegar. Simmer a second time until all the liquid has again evaporated. Refrigerate (this chutney will keep for one week).

Second Tack

Preparing the squid (Galley Pantry 1): Remove the heads and internal organs from the squid. Rinse thoroughly, taking care to leave the white sides of the squid intact. Slice the squid into thin rounds and rinse again. Set the slices of squid aside in a strainer so they will be as well drained as possible when ready to cook.

Third Tack

Fritter batter (Galley Pantry 2): Combine the flour, potato flour, baking powder, and Espelette pepper in a bowl. Gradually add the beer, beating constantly until the mixture is the consistency of crêpe batter. Heat the oil in the deep-fat fryer to 325°F (170°C).

Landfall

Scoop the chutney into four small ramekins.
Cooking the fritters: Transfer all the squid slices to the fritter batter. Stir gently with a fork. Remove the slices one by one from the bowl, shake off excess batter, and plunge into the hot oil in the deep-fat fryer. Fry until light blonde in color. Drain the squid on absorbent paper, season, and transfer to warm serving plates. Place a ramekin of chutney on the side of each plate. Serve.

Chutney

Galley Pantry 3
Tomato Chutney

This is prepared and marketed by Les Maisons de Bricourt
(see page 235).

3 lbs. (1.5 kg) tomatoes
1 large onion
3 medium cloves garlic
2 tbs olive oil
Mixed spices (from Galley Pantry 4)
¾ cup (20 cl) cider vinegar
1 tsp sugar

Galley Pantry 4
Mixed Spices

5 capsules green cardamom
1 tsp mace
2 cloves
1 tsp paprika
2 tbs (25 g) sugar

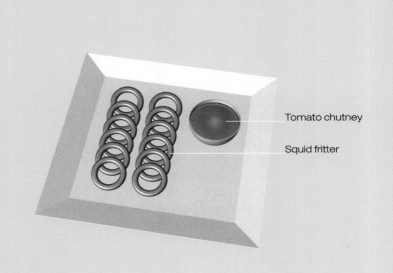

Tomato chutney

Squid fritter

Setting the Course—How can we duplicate the sensation of hot summer sun reflected from seaside cliffs and paths? The reason tomatoes have always seemed a perfect match for strawberries and raspberries is that they're distant cousins. The tomato is a fruit, too, and can hold its own with the most succulent of its relatives. For this stroll by the seaside, lemon and wild fennel apple lend a crisp acidulated note. The combination increases the complexity of the dish: each separate note enhances all the others.

Savory Tomatoes and Berries with

Crew of 4

Rigging
Airtight container
Nonstick baking sheet
Purée strainer
Japanese mandolin
Frying pan
Small bread pan
Small handheld blender
Sorbet maker
16 small sake bowls
4 large Burgundy wine glasses

Cruising Time
6 hours

From the Ship's Hold
Cerdon du Bugey Rosé

Provisions

Galley Pantry 1
Berry and Tomato Gazpacho
6 tomatoes
¼ lb. (125 g) strawberries
¼ lb. (125 g) raspberries
2 tbs sugar

Galley Pantry 2
Tomato Crisps
1 tomato
1 ¼ cup (300 g) sugar
1 cup (25 cl) water

July 24, 2003. No wind, dead calm. Early morning mist dissipated by noon.

First Tack

Berry and tomato gazpacho (Galley Pantry 1): Plunge the tomatoes for a few moments in boiling water, remove, peel, and seed. Place in a bowl with the strawberries, raspberries, and sugar. Blend these ingredients, using the handheld blender. Transfer the mixture to a purée strainer and strain, pressing well to extract as much pulp as possible. Refrigerate.

Second Tack

Tomato crisps (Galley Pantry 2): Use the Japanese mandolin to cut the tomato into wafer-thin slices. Bring the sugar and water to a boil and cook to the syrup stage. Remove from heat, cool to lukewarm, and add the sliced tomatoes. Allow the tomatoes to cool completely in the syrup, drain, and spread on a baking sheet covered with sheet of wax paper. Place the baking sheet in an oven heated to 200°F (90°C) and bake for 4 hours. Turn the tomatoes from time to time as they bake. When crisp, cool on a cake rack and store in an airtight container.

Third Tack

Lemon ice cream (Galley Pantry 3): Remove the zest from the lemons and squeeze the juice into a pot. Add one-half of the sugar to the lemon juice and lemon rind, bring to a boil. Beat the remaining lemon juice with the egg yolks. Combine all of these ingredients and cook over low heat, as for custard sauce. Strain, add the butter, and cool. When the mixture is cold, add the yogurt. Stir well and transfer to the sorbet maker. Store in freezer.

Fourth Tack

Semi-cooked tomatoes (Galley Pantry 4): Plunge the two tomatoes for a few seconds in boiling water, remove, and peel. Cut each peeled tomato into six wedges and remove the seeds. Sprinkle with salt, sugar, and pepper. Roll in the olive oil. Arrange the tomato wedges on a baking sheet without overlapping. Bake for 5 minutes in an oven heated to 320°F (160°C). Remove from oven and cool.

Fifth Tack

Preparation of the sake bowls (Galley Pantry 5): Cut the strawberries in two; leave the raspberries whole. Cut the semi-cooked tomatoes into small strips. Place some strawberries, raspberries, and three-quarters of the tomato strips in the sake bowls. Cover with the gazpacho.

Landfall

Pour the remaining berry gazpacho into the four wine glasses. Garnish with the semi-cooked tomato strips and a slice of tomato crisp. Garnish each of four sake bowls with 1 tsp lemon ice cream and a few sprigs of wild fennel apple (Galley Pantry 3). Serve.

Tangy Lemon and Wild Fennel Apple

Galley Pantry 3
Lemon Ice cream
5 lemons
1 cup (260 g) sugar
6 egg yolks
6 tbs (90 g) butter
½ cup (125 g) plain yogurt
A few sprigs wild fennel apple

Galley Pantry 4
Semi-Cooked Tomatoes
2 tomatoes
Salt
Sugar
White pepper
3 tbs olive oil

Galley Pantry 5
Garnish
12 whole raspberries
4 whole strawberries

Tomato crisp
Semi-cooked tomato
Gazpacho

Lemon ice cream
Gazpacho

Beans:
The versatile staple
latitude 12°3'0" S, longitude 77°2'60" W

Peru. Men first started growing and harvesting beans more than seven thousand years ago in Peru.

History
Men first started growing and harvesting beans more than seven thousand years ago in Peru. They were brought back to Europe by Christopher Columbus, who "discovered" them in Cuba. In fact, beans were already a staple foodstuff in both North and South America. The explorer Jacques Cartier also described beans in his account of his travels along the Saint Lawrence River.

In 1528, the pope ordered beans to be planted in Rome. He was rightly convinced that beans would prove a cheap and plentiful source of nourishment for the poorer inhabitants. When Catherine de Médicis married Henri II of France in 1533, she brought beans with her as part of her dowry. The first beans in France were planted in the august surroundings of the royal castle in Blois.

Runner beans only appeared in the early twentieth century in the eastern United States, where plant breeders carefully selected strains to produce the long, green beans.

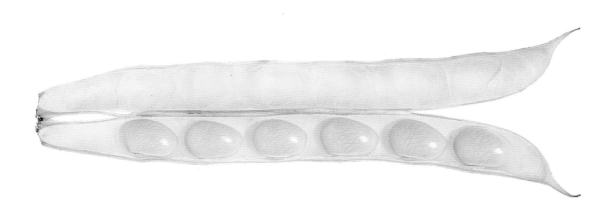

Natural history
Beans are legumes and members of the *Fabaceae* family. Centuries of selective breeding have led to the development of more than twelve thousand varieties. Beans can either be eaten "green," or in the form of seeds. Beans eaten in seed form, such as broad beans, have a more or less tough outer coating. The others, such as snow peas, are eaten pods and all.

Qualities
I love the flavor of beans, particularly the *Paimpolais coco* variety, which are slightly sweet and which melt in the mouth.

Uses
Every September I serve up semi-dried, deliciously tender coco beans with a pretty mother-of-pearl color skin. I like to add a piece of seaweed such as kombu to flavor the beans while they are cooking. You should only add salt at the very end, otherwise the skins become tough. I also like to cook them until they are very soft, then drain them and blend them with a squeeze of lemon juice, a dribble of cream, and a touch of spice. The result is a light, tasty bean salsa that can be served with a dash of Italian olive oil. Another favorite of mine is to serve a salad of cold coco beans with a few Bouchot mussels and strips of pepper in a nicely acid vinaigrette. Runner beans need to be cooked just right. If they are not cooked for long enough their delicate taste does not have time to develop.

The finest beans
The best seed beans are coco beans from Paimpol in Brittany. I can recommend three varieties of pod beans—butter beans, saint-fiacre, and striped green beans.

Health benefits
Runner beans are rich in minerals, antioxidants, and vitamins. They help protect against the signs of aging and against cardiovascular disease.Dried beans are very rich in proteins, trace elements, and minerals. They can help lower cholesterol and are recommended for patients with diabetes.

Setting the Course—As the sun sets on a fine summer's day in Brittany, I dream of following the golden orb across the sea to the birthplace of the humble bean. To satisfy this wanderlust of mine, I season my own Paimpol or Cancale beans with a blend of spices inspired by even more exotic climes—the coast of the Red Sea, with its medley of Middle-Eastern accents. September marks one of the year's most important events, the arrival of royal prawns on the rock faces. We trap the prawns in lobster pots or scoop them up with nets at high tide. I've always been intrigued by the distinctive taste of the gold-tinged shells, and this gave me the idea of using them to make an aromatic oil.

First Tack
The night before, prepare the vanilla oil (Galley Pantry 1). Split the vanilla bean lengthwise and cut the two halves in half again. Place in the Mason jar and add the grape-seed oil. Close tightly and sterilize in a boiling water bath, counting 10 minutes from second boil. Cool and refrigerate until the next day. Preparing the beans (Galley Pantry 2): The night before, peel and rinse the whole onion, carrot, and garlic cloves. Tie together a bouquet garni containing the celery rib, the green half-leek, sprigs of thyme, and bay leaf. Rinse the navy beans, place in pot, and cover with water to a depth of 1 in. (2 cm) above the beans. Bring to a boil and skim. Add the vegetables, bouquet garni, and peppercorns. Simmer for 30 to 40 minutes, depending on the freshness of the beans. Add salt midway through cooking—adding salt sooner will harden the outside of the beans. Remove from heat and allow to cool in the cooking liquid. Refrigerate until the next day.

Royal Prawns and Creamed Navy Be

Crew of 4

Rigging
Small, handheld blender
Strainer
Mason jar
Coffee mill
4 soup plates

Cruising Time
24 hours

From the Ship's Hold
Chablis Grand Cru

Provisions

Galley Pantry 1
Vanilla Oil
1 vanilla bean (pod)
½ cup (⅛ liter) grape-seed oil

Finishing
½ cup (⅛ liter) cream

Galley Pantry 2
Pot Herbs
1 lb. (400 g) fresh, shelled navy beans
1 onion
1 carrot
3 cloves garlic
1 rib celery
½ leek, green portion only
1 bay leaf
3 sprigs thyme
5 black peppercorns

September 10, 2001. Wind from the northeast, force 2. Sparkling sea; good visibility.

Second Tack

The night before, prepare the exotic spice mixture (Galley Pantry 3). Roast the sesame and cumin seeds in a dry frying pan until golden. Allow to cool completely. Place the cardamom, ajowan, oregano, and cooled sesame and cumin seeds in the coffee mill. Pulverize these ingredients and set aside. Place the sumac in the coffee mill and pulverize as finely as possible, then add the ground cinnamon. Grind again, add the first mixture, and grind again. Transfer all these ingredients to an airtight container.

Third Tack

Three hours before serving, prepare the prawn oil (Galley Pantry 4). First, cook the prawns in 1 quart (1 liter) water seasoned with salt (1 generous tbs, or 20 grams) and pepper. Rinse the prawns in cold water, drain, and shell. Set aside 12 prawns with their heads for the final garnish. Remove the remaining heads and place with all the shells in a pot containing 1 tbs heated sunflower oil. Sauté the shells and heads until stiff and fragrant. Crush with a fork, add the remaining sunflower oil. Heat the oil to 212°F (100°C), remove from heat and steep for 1 hour before straining.

Fourth Tack

Lastly, prepare the creamed navy beans (Galley Pantry 2). Drain the beans, reserving all the cooking liquid. Remove the pot herbs. Place the beans and cream (Galley Pantry 1) in a large pot, and cover with the cooking liquid from the beans. Reheat slowly, transfer to blender, blend and then strain. If too thick, dilute with a little of the bean cooking liquid. Set aside and keep warm.

Landfall

Warm four soup plates. Reheat the creamed navy beans, dilute if necessary with a little of the cooking liquid. Reheat all the prawns briefly in 3 tbs prawn oil. Arrange the headless prawns in the soup plates. Whip the creamed beans with the blender and transfer to the soup plates. Place the reserved prawns with heads on the edges of each soup plate. Run a line of the exotic spice mixture around the prawn garnish and over the creamed beans. Sprinkle a little of the vanilla oil over the line of exotic spice mixture and dot with prawn oil. Serve.

ans Accented with an Exotic Spice Mixture

Galley Pantry 3
Exotic Spice Mixture

This mixture is available ready-to-use from Les Maisons de Bricourt (see Poudre du Voyage, page 234). Proportions are a guide only, as amounts depend on the quality and origin of each spice.

3 tbs sesame seeds
1 tbs cumin seeds
1 tbs cardamom capsules
1 tbs ajowan seeds
1 tbs dried oregano
2 tbs sumac
1 tbs ground cinnamon

Galley Pantry 4
Prawn Oil

80 live prawns
½ cup (12 cl) sunflower oil

Whole prawns

Creamed beans

Exotic spice mixture
Prawn oil
Vanilla oil

Setting the Course—When I first invented my "Grande Caravane" powder, I intended it as an accompaniment for the salt-meadow lamb that grazes on the "steppes" below Mont-Saint-Michel. Today I've rediscovered it as an accompaniment for mullet, that "woodcock" of the sea. The powder is even better when a hint of Niora pepper is added. The lightly cooked navy beans provide a perfect backdrop for the combination of simplicity and character afforded by the ground spices and the tangy taste of the mullet.

Mullet "Grande Caravane" with Brais

134

Crew of 4

Rigging
Coffee mill
Nonstick frying pan
Strainer
4 plates

Cruising Time
4 hours

From the Ship's Hold
Red Pessac-Léognan or Red Côtes-de-Provence

Provisions

Galley Pantry 1
8 mullet weighing a generous 4 oz. (150 g) each
1 tbs sunflower oil
1 generous tbs (20 g) salted butter
1 tsp "Grande Caravane" Powder (see Galley Pantry 4)

Galley Pantry 2
Garnish
1 lb. (400 g) Paimpol navy beans
¾ cup (20 cl) chicken bouillon
1 clove garlic
1 small onion
1 sprig thyme
Rind of 1 orange
2 tomatoes

August 30, 2004. Wind from the west, force 2 to 3. Sparkling sea, good visibility, high-altitude cumulus clouds.

First Tack

Preparing the fish (Galley Pantry 1): Carefully scale and clean the mullet, retaining the livers. Set the fish and livers aside.

Second Tack

"Grande Caravane" powder (Galley Pantry 4): In a dry pan, lightly roast the cardamom, sesame, and cumin to release the fragrances. Add the remaining spices and grind in coffee mill. Store in a jar.

Third Tack

Preparing the garnish (Galley Pantry 2): Simmer the navy beans with the chicken bouillon, garlic clove, onion, sprig of thyme, and orange rind until soft but not mushy. Cool the beans in the cooking liquid. Plunge the tomatoes briefly in boiling water, remove, peel, seed, and cut into quarters.

Fourth Tack

Preparing the juice (Galley Pantry 3): Slice the shallot, and chop the garlic and parsley. Sauté the mullet livers in 1 scant tbs (10 g) butter. Add the shallot, garlic and 1 tbs "Grande Caravane" powder. Cover these ingredients with the sherry vinegar and chicken bouillon. Bring to a boil and reduce by one-half. Add 3 tbs (50 g) butter and the chopped parsley. Mix with the blender. Strain, pressing to extract as much of the juice as possible. Set aside.

Landfall

Drain the navy beans and reheat. Add the tomatoes and simmer for about 10 minutes. Season the mullets with salt and the "Grande Caravane" spices. Sauté with the butter and oil in a nonstick frying pan until golden (4 minutes on each side). Reheat the juice while whipping constantly. Place two whole mullets in each of four large warmed plates. Add the cooking liquid from the navy beans and garnish with a row of beans. Serve the juice (Galley Pantry 3) in a gravy boat on the side. Diners should first remove the bones from their fish, and then serve themselves sauce from the gravy boat.

ed Navy Beans

Galley Pantry 3
Juice
1 shallot
½ clove garlic
A few sprigs parsley
1 tbs "Grande Caravane" powder
1 tsp sherry vinegar
10 cl chicken bouillon
1 tbs + 3 tbs (10 g + 50 g) butter

Galley Pantry 4
"Grande Caravane" Powder
This mixture is available ready-to-use from Les Maisons de Bricourt (see page 234). Proportions given are a guide only, since amounts depend on the quality and origin of each spice.
2 tbs green cardamom capsules
2 tbs cumin
2 tbs golden sesame
2 tbs fenugreek seeds
1 tsp ground cinnamon
5 cloves
2 tbs ground Niora powder
1 nutmeg
5 tbs sweet paprika

Juice

Navy beans

Mullet

Artichoke: The bitter Flower
latitude 37°58'60" N, longitude 23°43'60" E

Europe. Artichokes as we know them today are the result of two thousand years of careful selective breeding, by gardeners who saw the potential in this variety of thistle.

History

Artichokes as we know them today are the result of two thousand years of careful selective breeding, by gardeners who saw the potential in this variety of thistle.

The ancient Greeks were very fond of wild thistles. The Romans loved them so much that they established thistle farms and sold their produce at high prices. After the fall of the Roman Empire in the fifth century C.E., thistles were no longer harvested in Europe, although they were still cultivated across the Mediterranean, in Carthage, in modern-day Tunisia. When the Arabs conquered Andalusia, Spain, in the eighth century C.E., they brought the thistles back with them. Over the centuries, the strains were carefully selected to produce what we now know as the artichoke.

Artichokes spread to Italy in the thirteenth century. At one of the many fairs or markets where plants and seedlings changed hands, often for high prices, a French merchant acquired some artichoke seeds. The plants gradually spread across France and into northern Europe—although it is not certain that a modern consumer would have recognized them as the artichokes we know today.

During the Renaissance, when all of Europe looked to Italy as a model of refinement, artichokes once again became highly fashionable among the aristocracy. It was not until much later that seeds were transplanted from the walled gardens of the wealthy to the open fields farmed by the peasants. Artichokes were very popular during the nineteenth century. However, they seem to have fallen out of favor since the 1960s, although Spain and Italy still export vast quantities of artichokes every year. Nowadays, artichokes have also crossed the Atlantic and are harvested in California, Argentina, and Chile.

Natural history

An artichoke is a flower, or to be more precise a group of flowerets, growing on a fleshy base known as the heart. Artichokes grow on thick, woody stems that can reach up to nearly five feet (1.5 meters) in height. The leaves, which show that the plant is a member of the composite flower family, are long and jagged and sometimes end in a sharp point.

Qualities

Sweet and bitter at the same time, and never too rich.

I particularly like the mineral, slightly hazelnutty, even metallic taste of the juice, and am always pleasantly surprised by the balance of flavors. The scent of the flower reminds me of honey and almonds.

Uses

Like asparagus, artichokes are a problem when it comes to choosing a suitable wine. Artichoke hearts are delicious blended with poultry bouillon and served with a splash of hazelnut oil.

The finest artichokes

One of the finest varieties of artichoke is the Camus, grown in Brittany. I like nothing better than to tear off its leaves and dip them in a tasty cider-vinegar vinaigrette, until I reach the tender and succulent heart.

Artichokes are an excellent accompaniment for fish and shellfish.

Health benefits

The compounds that give artichokes their bitter taste are concentrated in the roots and the leaves. They have a depurative (purifying) quality that was known to the Greeks and Romans, and which makes them especially suitable for people with a high cholesterol level or who are suffering from gout. The same depurative compounds mean that artichokes can be used to treat skin problems such as eczema and rashes.

Artichokes are also particularly rich in trace elements, including potassium and calcium. They also contain a rare carbohydrate called inulin, also found in Jerusalem artichokes, which is recommended for diabetics. Artichokes are also known to be beneficial for the liver. They should be eaten as soon as they are cooked, otherwise they become difficult to digest.

Setting the Course—To complement the crisp freshness of the mullet—an extremely delicate fish considered peerless by many connoisseurs—I invented an aromatic bouillon. A wild creature such as mullet, accustomed as it is to the billowy wave, is never better than when pitted against a full-bodied tafia—the seafarer's rum. Here we have an exceptional bouillon accented with a Seafood Spice Mixture that blends subtly with the iodine of the mullet and bitterness of the artichoke.

First Tack

Prepare the Niora oil (Galley Pantry 3) the night before—at the latest. Crush the Niora peppers and transfer to a Mason jar. Add the grape-seed oil and annatto seeds. Close the jar tightly and sterilize in a water bath for 10 minutes after second boil. Cool the jar unopened in the water bath until the next day, strain the contents, and set aside.

Second Tack

Preparing the eggplant-and-mullet purée (Galley Pantry 5): Rinse the eggplant, remove the stem end, cut in two lengthwise, and slash in one or two places to hasten cooking. Wrap the eggplant in aluminum foil and cook for

two hours in an oven heated to 300°F (150°C). Preparing the seafood spice mixture (Galley Pantry 2): Roast all the spices except the oregano in a frying pan for a few minutes. Cool and grind with the dried oregano in the coffee mill. Set aside.

Third Tack

Cooking the artichokes (Galley Pantry 4): Place the water, juice of one-half lemon, coriander seeds, olive oil, salt, and sugar in a pot. Squeeze the remaining one and a half lemons into a small bowl. Using a sharp knife, trim all the leaves off the artichokes, leaving only the hearts. Plunge the artichoke hearts immediately into the bowl of lemon juice to

Baby Mullet with Tafia, the Seafarer's

Crew of 4	Provisions	Galley Pantry 3
		Stock for the Mullet
Rigging	**Galley Pantry 1**	12 mullet bones and heads
Small handheld	24 small mullets	1 clove garlic
blender	Olive oil	1 new onion
Strainer	Salt and pepper	2 tbs olive oil
Mason jar		1 sprig thyme
Oven with broiler	**Galley Pantry 2**	2 tbs sherry vinegar
Coffee mill	Seafood Spice Mixture	2 tbs white Port
Pastry brush	*This mixture is available ready-to-use from*	2 cups (½ liter) water
4 bowls	*Les Maisons de Bricourt (see Poudre Marine,*	
	page 234). Proportions are a guide only, since	**Tafia Sauce**
Cruising Time	*amounts depend on the quality and origin*	½ cup (12 cl) cooking liquid from the
24 hours	*of each spice.*	artichokes
	1 tsp ajowan seeds	1 tbs + 1 tbs rum
From the Ship's	3 tsp cumin seeds	Rind of 2 lemons
Hold	1 tsp white peppercorns	1 sprig fresh oregano
Palette Blanc	2 tsp fennel seeds	1½ tbs (20 g) butter
	2 tsp dried oregano	1 tsp Seafood Spice Mixture (see Galley
		Pantry 2)

June 22, 2003. Wind from the west, force 2 to 3. Light breeze; good visibility.

prevent them from discoloring. Transfer the artichoke hearts to the mixture in the pot, bring to a boil, reduce the heat, and simmer for about 30 minutes. Test for doneness with the tip of a knife. Remove the artichoke hearts from the cooking liquid, cut in half, scoop out the choke, and return to the cooking liquid. Set aside.

Fourth Tack

Preparing the mullet (Galley Pantry 1): Scale and rinse the fish. Cut out the fillets and remove the bones. Spread a baking sheet with the olive oil, sprinkle with salt and pepper. Place the fillets on the baking dish, skin-side up, and use the pastry brush to cover them with olive oil. The mullet is now ready to cook. Finishing the eggplant-and-mullet purée (Galley Pantry 5): Using a tablespoon, scrape as much of the cooked eggplant pulp as possible into a bowl. Sauté the mullet livers in a small pan with the olive oil, add the sherry vinegar, and scrape to deglaze the pan. Add the eggplant pulp. Transfer this mixture to a bowl and blend, using the handheld blender. When well blended, strain, pressing well to extract as much of the mixture as possible. Set aside.

Fifth Tack

Mullet stock and Tafia sauce (Galley Pantry 3): Preparing the mullet stock: heat the olive oil in a pot over high heat, add the 12 fish bones and heads and allow to color, stirring constantly. Add the garlic clove, chopped onion, and sprig of thyme. Deglaze the pot with the sherry vinegar and white Port. Add the water, bring to the boil, reduce the heat, and simmer for about 45 minutes. Strain.

There should be about 1 cup (25 cl) of stock. Finishing the Tafia sauce (Galley Pantry 3): Place half a cup (12 cl) of the artichoke cooking liquid in a pot. Add the mullet stock, 1 tbs of the rum, the lemon rinds, sprig of oregano, and 1 tbs of the seafood spice mixture. Bring these ingredients to a boil and reduce by one-half. Strain, beat in the butter, and add the remaining tablespoon of rum. Rectify the seasoning and set aside.

Landfall

Preheat the broiler. Reheat the artichoke hearts in the remaining cooking liquid. Reheat the eggplant-and-mullet purée in a double boiler over boiling water. Reheat the Tafia sauce. Place the baking sheet with the mullets about 4 in. (10 cm) below the broiler grill and cook for 3 to 4 minutes. Remove the baking sheet from the oven and arrange the fillets in twos to resemble the original fish. On four large, warmed soup plates, arrange three artichoke halves on one side, three reassembled mullets on the other. Scoop a little of the eggplant-and-mullet purée onto the plates above the fish, sprinkle with the puffed quinoa seeds. Scatter the leek sprouts and oregano leaves beside the artichokes. Beat the Tafia sauce until emulsified, and pour over the fish. Dot the sauce with a few teaspoons of the Niora oil. Serve.

Rum

Niora Oil
This oil is available from Les Maisons de Bricourt (see page 234).
1 scant cup (10 cl) grape-seed oil
3 tsp annatto seeds
4 Niora (small round, dried peppers)

Galley Pantry 4
Artichoke
10 small "Camus" artichokes
2 cups (50 cl) water
2 lemons
10 coriander seeds
5 tbs olive oil
½ tsp salt
2 pinches sugar

Galley Pantry 5
Eggplant-and-Mullet Purée
2 small eggplants
Livers from the mullet

1 tbs olive oil
1 tbs sherry vinegar

Galley Pantry 6
A few leaves golden oregano
A few puffed quinoa seeds

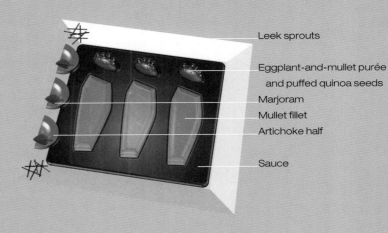

Leek sprouts

Eggplant-and-mullet purée
    and puffed quinoa seeds

Marjoram

Mullet fillet

Artichoke half

Sauce

Setting the Course—I constructed this recipe like a fable, with all the trappings—including a moral. There's a cast of characters, of course: the artichoke, the scallop, the apple. And each of them has a distinctive personality, reflecting our perception of their individual impact, properties, and taste. Two outsiders not listed with my cast of main characters play supporting roles that may be minor but are nonetheless crucial. These are the foie gras and the angelica. The moral of this fable comes to us from Lionel Poilâne, who said, "No one should ever consider greed a sin."

Artichokes, Scallops, and Apple

148

Crew of 4	Provisions
Rigging	**Galley Pantry 1**
Small, handheld blender	6 medium scallops per person (24 in all)
Nonstick frying pan	
Japanese mandolin	**Galley Pantry 2**
Mason jar	**Sauce**
12 small wooden skewers	2 oz. (50 g) foie gras
4 plates	2 tbs cider vinegar
	½ Granny Smith apple
Cruising Time	4 tbs apple juice
48 hours	10 tbs grape-seed oil
	1 tbs egg white
From the Ship's Hold	
White Saumur or Saint-Aubin	

October 2002. Wind from the southwest, force 3 to 4. Fairly calm sea, rain, and poor visibility.

First Tack

Forty-eight hours in advance, prepare the angelica oil (Galley Pantry 3). Chop the angelica and transfer to a small Mason jar with the grape-seed oil. Close tightly, place in a boiling water bath, and sterilize for 10 minutes after the second boil.

Second Tack

Prepare the sauce (Galley Pantry 2) shortly before serving. Sauté the seasoned foie gras briefly, deglaze the pan with the cider vinegar, and scrape the contents of the pan into a large bowl. Peel, seed, and dice the apple, and add to the other ingredients in the bowl. Add the apple juice, grape-seed oil, and egg white. Blend thoroughly with handheld blender and strain, pressing well to extract all the liquid. Transfer to a pot and set aside.

Third Tack

Shell the scallops (Galley Pantry 1) or ask your fish seller to do it for you. Rinse the shelled scallops and drain on absorbent paper. Two hours before serving, sauté the scallops on one side in a nonstick frying pan. Spear 2 scallops on each skewer, cooked side facing out. Place in a single row on a baking pan.

Fourth Tack

Preparing the artichokes (Galley Pantry 4): Place the grape-seed oil and juice of 2 lemons in a bowl. Trim the leaves off the artichokes and remove the hearts. Scrape the chokes out of the trimmed hearts and discard. As you work, rub the artichoke hearts with the remaining lemon, cut in halves, to prevent discoloration. Cut the artichoke hearts into very thin slices and place in the bowl of lemon juice and grape-seed oil. Heat a nonstick frying pan. Transfer the sliced artichoke hearts to the hot pan and sauté. Work in small batches so the slices do not overlap. Transfer the cooked artichoke slices to a pot. Use the Japanese mandolin to cut the radishes and apple (Galley Pantry 4) into thin julienne strips. Chop these strips into matchsticks. Sprinkle the apple with a little lemon juice to prevent discoloration. Add the chervil leaves and 2 tsp angelica oil. Set this mixture aside at room temperature.

Landfall

Preheat oven for 30 minutes to 350°F (180°C). Bake the skewered scallops for 6 to 8 minutes. Reheat the artichokes. Heat the sauce, whipping constantly, but do not allow to boil. When the scallops are cooked, remove the skewers. Place a row of artichoke-heart strips on each plate and top with the scallops, transparent side up. Fill the empty spaces on the plate generously with sauce. Garnish each scallop with the shredded apple-and-radish mixture. Dot the sauce with angelica oil and serve.

Galley Pantry 3
Angelica Oil
1 freshly cut sprig angelica
½ cup (12 cl) grape-seed oil

Galley Pantry 4
Garnish
8 large artichokes
2 + 1 lemons
5 tbs grape-seed oil
20 large round radishes
1 Granny Smith apple
5 sprigs chervil
2 tsp angelica oil (from Galley Pantry 3)

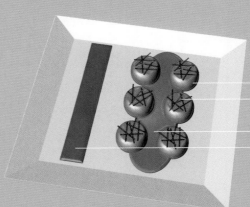

Scallops
Apple-and-radish garnish

Sauce and angelica oil
Artichoke-heart strips

Coffee: The stimulant
latitude 13°19'13" N, longitude 43°15'16" E

Yemen, Ethiopia. Over the course of five centuries, sailors, planters, and traders have taken this African shrub all over the world.

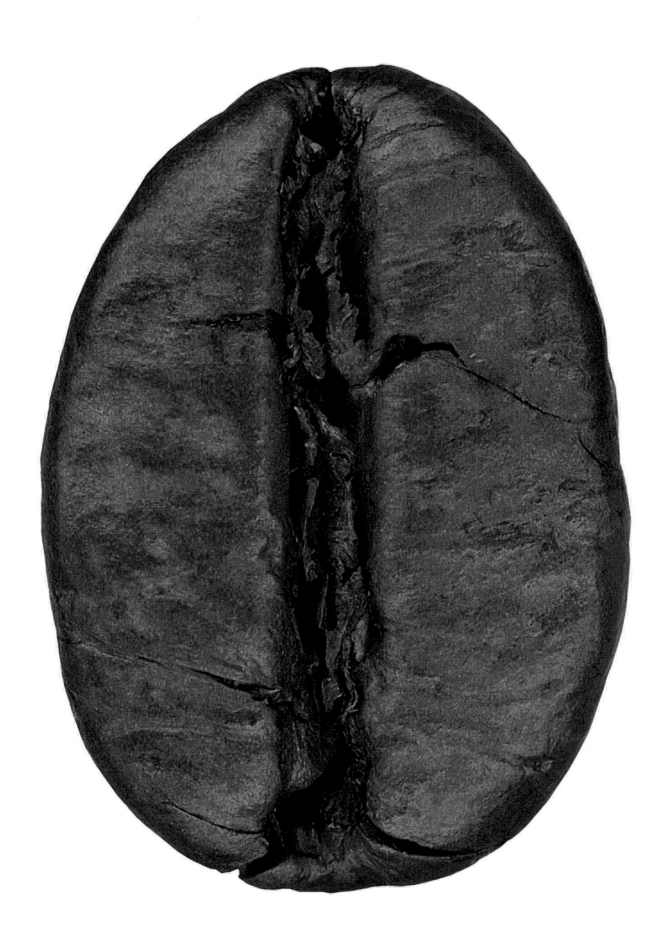

History

Over the course of five centuries, sailors, planters, and traders have taken this African shrub all over the world. Legend has it that coffee was discovered by a Yemeni goatherd named Kaldi, who noticed that his goats would not sleep after eating the red berries of one particular shrub. The berries were, of course, coffee beans. The story then goes that an Ethiopian monk started giving the beans to his fellow monks so that they would stay awake during the long hours of prayer. The coffee trade began in the small port of Mocha in Yemen. From there, the taste for coffee spread throughout Arabia, Egypt, Persia, Turkey, and India.

In 1616, a Dutchman named Pieter van der Broccke managed to steal some coffee beans, which he planted in the greenhouses of the botanical gardens in Amsterdam. He stole the beans in Mocha, by then a major international trading center for coffee. This was quite a feat, considering that the Arabs were so determined to hang on to their monopoly that they only allowed roasted coffee beans to be loaded on ships so that there could be no chance of them germinating. The great European trading companies bought their supplies in Mocha until the mid-seventeenth century, when the Dutch began planting their own coffee in Ceylon, southern India, and Indonesia.

The earliest known coffeehouses were opened in Istanbul by two merchants, Djems de Damasco and Hakim de Alepo. In the middle of the seventeenth century, Arab merchants introduced coffee to Venice. According to historians, the first European café opened in Saint Mark's Square in 1645. From Venice, coffee was exported to London, where the first recorded coffeehouse opened in 1652. It was run by an Italian.

Remarkably, espresso machines date back to 1822, while instant coffee was invented by a scientist working in Chicago in 1901. Coffee filters were invented in 1908 by Melitta Bentz, a German housewife. Today, coffee is one of the world's favorite beverages.

Natural history
Coffee is made from the roasted beans of a shrub of the *Rubiaceae* family. It comes in two varieties: arabica *(Coffea arabica)* and robusta *(Coffea canephora)*.

Qualities
Robusta has a very high caffeine content and a powerful, even bitter taste.

Arabica is smooth, fruity, and spicy, with overtones of chocolate and a slightly acid bite. Its aroma can be astonishingly complex.

Uses
Coffee is prepared in a variety of different ways around the world. Every region favors their own method, whether it be the steaming mug of rather weak coffee enjoyed by the British or the concentrated caffeine kick of a tiny cup of black Turkish coffee. In Yemen, people like to sprinkle their coffee with pepper, while in the Middle East it is often flavored with cardamom.

Specialist coffee roasters select the finest beans to produce a coffee that is full-bodied, dense, full of flavor, rich in aroma, and with a well-balanced, harmonious taste. There are an infinite variety of combinations, and the subtle differences between one blend and another are often simply a question of personal taste.

Coffee is also widely used in desserts, either alone or along with sugar and chocolate. In the eighteenth century, chefs experimented with marrying coffee with ingredients such as vanilla, sugar, and cacao. They came up with a range of desserts and pastries that are still very popular today, including coffee creams, eclairs, profiteroles, mochas, ice creams, and candies.

Coffee is rarely used in savory dishes. It can be used in spice mixes to flavor poultry or white meats. I love nothing better than experimenting with unusual combinations of ingredients, and among my more successful efforts have been coffee with seafood, particularly in the nage sauce for crayfish with chervil and roasted coffee.

The finest coffees
I always prefer arabica to robusta, which is too overpowering for my taste. Coffee grows best in tropical regions at a medium altitude. The quality depends very much on the altitude, in fact. The higher the altitude of the plantation, the better the coffee, as the beans ripen more slowly.

I have a number of favorite arabicas. For breakfast, my favorite is an Ethiopian mocha called Harrar, which is mild and fruity. After lunch, I prefer the more powerful and deeper-tasting Djimmah, while in the evening I drink Sidamo or Limu, two varieties that are mild, flavorful, and low in caffeine. I also recommend Sanani, which is a wild-tasting, spicy mocha from Yemen. Another two favorites are the deliciously acid, fruity coffees from Kenya, and the chocolaty Blue Mountain from Jamaica, widely held to be one of the finest coffees in the world. Whenever I am traveling in India, I drink Mysore and Malabar, which are powerful, spicy, and acid. Coffee from Costa Rica is full-flavored and has a rich aroma. On chilly winter evenings, nothing is more warming than a mild, smooth cup of Colombian with a drop or two of fine rum.

True coffee lovers should taste the very mild, smooth, and slightly peppery beans from Hawaii and the sweet, harmonious, chocolaty coffee from Papua New Guinea.

Health benefits
Coffee is well known as a stimulant.

Setting the Course—First thing in the morning in every Breton or Norman bistro, you would find sea-dogs and land-lubbers alike kick-starting their day with a splash of apple eau-de-vie, coarse and strong, in the bottom of their coffee cup. This aroma of coffee and calvados—called *mic* here, for some reason—remains engraved in my memory, imbued with the more bitter and rough odor of gray rolling tobacco. What stories, what voyages, what adventures did they sit and share? I have tried to envisage at what moment that meeting between coffee, from the faraway port of Mocha, and the local apple eau-de-vie might have come about. The story is probably close to that of Irish coffee. . . .

Calvados Coffee

154

Crew of 4	Provisions
Rigging	**Galley Pantry 1**
Small handheld blender	Apple Ice
Ice-crusher	2 Granny Smith apples
Mason jar	½ lemon
4 gauze squares	4 tsp water
8 liqueur glasses	
	Galley Pantry 2
Cruising Time	Spiced Concentrated Coffee
24 hours	4 tsp ground coffee
	1 tsp powdered cinnamon
	4 green cardamom pods
	½ cup (12 cl) water
	½ cup (100 g) glucose
	1 tsp coffee extract
	1 tbs calvados

June 29, 2004. Light southerly breeze, force 2. Visibility good, sea calm.

First Tack

Prepare the apple ice (Galley Pantry 1) a day in advance. Peel one of the apples. Cut both apples into 8 pieces and remove the core. Slice finely and add the lemon juice and water. Mix well. Place in freezer until next day. Spiced concentrated coffee (Galley Pantry 2): Place the ground coffee, powdered cinnamon, and crushed cardamom pods into the Mason jar. Mix the water, glucose, and coffee extract in a pan. Bring to the boil and pour into the jar. Set aside until the next day.

Second Tack

On the day of the meal, sterilize and unfold the gauze squares and filter the contents of the Mason jar through them. Add the calvados (Galley Pantry 2). Put the iced apple through the ice-crusher and distribute it evenly between 4 liqueur glasses. Keep in freezer until 30 minutes before the meal, at most. Pour one-third of the coffee concentrate into the 4 remaining glasses, and store in freezer with the apple glasses.

Third Tack

White chocolate milk (Galley Pantry 3): Prepare two double-boiler pans, one hot and one cold. Heat the water in the hot one to 195°F (90°C), and put cold water and ice cubes in the cold one. Place the milk and white chocolate over the hot pan. Stir regularly, and when the chocolate has melted, whisk briskly to form a froth. Spoon off the froth from the surface and transfer it to the cooling pan. Repeat the whisking-skimming operation 5 or 6 times. Keep the froth very cold, and keep the chocolate milk warm.

Landfall

First take the four glasses containing apple out of the freezer. Pour ¼ in. (0.5 cm) of spiced concentrated coffee into each glass, then share out the cold froth. Take out the remaining glasses containing the coffee concentrate and gently pour onto the white chocolate milk: the concentrate should not mix in completely. Serve.

Galley Pantry 3
White Chocolate Milk

3½ oz. (100 g) white chocolate
½ cup (12 cl) milk

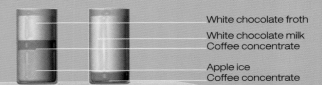

White chocolate froth
White chocolate milk
Coffee concentrate

Apple ice
Coffee concentrate

Setting the Course—The remarkable meeting between the coffee bean from the Yemen and the green pods of cardamom from the Western Gaths mountains near Kerala, southern India, can probably be traced back to very ancient times. Some say that the first encounter happened in the middle of a desert: a nomad stopped his caravan to make coffee and unwittingly dropped some cardamom pods into the scalding brew. Since then, in many cultures, coffee and cardamom have become inseparable. Over the centuries people have learned how to vary their proportions and find the perfect blend between these two seeds, different though their flavors are.

Coffee Soufflé and Cardamom Marsh

Crew of 4

Rigging
Airtight container
Candy thermometer
4 soufflé molds, 4 in. (10 cm) in diameter
Flexible spatula
Small "Kitchenaid"-type blender
Baking tin 10 x 8 in. (26 x 20 cm), 2 in. (5 cm) high
4 plates

Cruising Time
24 hours

From the Ship's Hold
15 year-old Verdelho Madeira

Provisions

Galley Pantry 1
Coffee Custard
1 cup (25 cl) milk
2 tbs sugar
2 egg yolks
4 tbs cornstarch
6 tsp coffee extract

Galley Pantry 2
Cardamom Marshmallow
4 tbs agar-agar (seaweed gelatin)
6 tbs (9 cl) water
2 tbs (40 g) glucose
2 cups (440 g) sugar
¼ cup (55 g) egg whites
1 ½ tsp freshly-ground cardamom
2 tbs powdered cocoa

March 15, 2004. Breeze from the southwest, force 4 to 5. Overcast; sea rough.

First Tack

Coffee custard (Galley Pantry 1): Add half the sugar to the milk and bring to boil. Combine the rest of the sugar with the egg yolks, cornstarch, and coffee extract. Whisk a little of the hot milk into this mixture. Pour back into the remaining hot milk and cook the custard until it reaches boiling point, whisking constantly. Cool.

Second Tack

Cardamom marshmallow (Galley Pantry 2): First prepare the marshmallow dusting: mix the cornstarch and confectioner's sugar and sprinkle into the tin, covering the bottom. Dissolve the agar-agar in a tablespoon of warm water. Place the sugar, glucose, and water in a pan, bring to boil and continue to cook. Meanwhile, start whisking the egg whites in the blender. When the sugar and glucose syrup has reached hard-ball stage, or 265°F (130°C) on a candy thermometer, add it to the egg whites, continuing to whisk. Add the agar-agar and the powdered cardamom. Allow to cool while continuing to whisk. Pour the mixture into the tin and spread it out evenly. Sprinkle with the cornstarch-sugar mix. Cover with plastic wrap and leave to dry out for 24 hours. Cut the marshmallow into ½ in. (1.5 cm) cubes. Store in an airtight container.

Third Tack

Soufflé (Galley Pantry 3): Butter the soufflé molds and sprinkle with sugar. Whisk the egg whites with a few drops of lemon juice. When frothy, fold in the sugar a little at a time. Start to warm the custard while whisking. When the egg whites are stiff, whisk a quarter of them into the custard. Then fold in the rest delicately with the spatula. Pour the mixture into the soufflé molds, filling them up to three-quarters full. Preheat the oven to 350°F (180°C) and cook the soufflés for 5 minutes.

Landfall

Using large, square plates, place the cooked soufflé on the right of the plate and 3 cubes of marshmallow to one side. Sprinkle with cocoa powder (Galley Pantry 2) and serve.

mallow

Marshmallow Dusting
⅓ cup (50 g) cornstarch
⅓ cup (50 g) confectioner's sugar

Galley Pantry 3
Soufflé
⅔ cup (150 g) egg whites
A few drops of lemon juice
2 tbs sugar
1 ½ cups (200 g) coffee custard from Galley Pantry 1

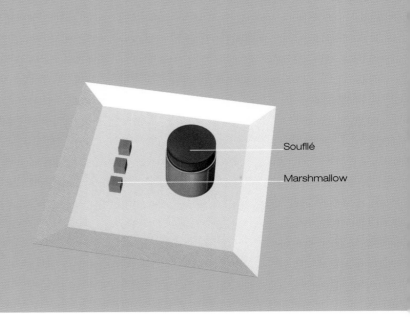

Soufflé

Marshmallow

Cacao:
The sweet temptation
latitude 15°7'60" N, longitude 87°28'0" W

Honduras. The Mayans are known to have cultivated cacao in what is now Mexico as early as 1500 B.C.E.

History

The Mayans are known to have cultivated cacao in what is now Mexico as early as 1500 B.C.E. The first European to taste a drink made from cacao beans was Christopher Columbus, when he weighed anchor at the island of Guanaja, off the coast of Honduras, in 1502. Seventeen years later, Cortez arrived at the same destination. One of the first welcoming gifts he received from the Aztec emperor was a vast cacao plantation. The Aztecs fermented and then dried the beans before grinding them into powder. They mixed the powder with water and added dried chili peppers before heating the liquid until it frothed. To mark special occasions they added aniseed, annatto, vanilla, and wild honey, thickening the drink with a small amount of ground maize.

The Spanish conquistadors planted fields of sugar cane, which was soon used to sweeten the rather bitter drink. The first cacao was exported from Veracruz in Mexico and reached Spain in 1585. The demand for cacao was such that plantations were quickly established in San Domingo, Jamaica, Martinique, the Philippines, Brazil, and Trinidad and Tobago. The first cacao shrubs were planted in Africa in 1822.

Cacao became incredibly fashionable in Europe in the seventeenth century in the form of hot chocolate. It arrived in France in 1615 when Anne of Austria brought her own chocolate-makers to the court of Louis XIII. From there, chocolate reached London in 1657. Most cacao arrived in Europe via the port of Amsterdam.

Chocolate only became popular among the population as a whole as a result of the Industrial Revolution, when it became much more widely accessible.

Natural history

Cacao beans come from the pod of a small tree that grows best in shady conditions, *Theobroma cacao*, which is a member of the *Sterculiaceae* family. When the beans are ripe, they are fermented, washed, dried, and roasted.

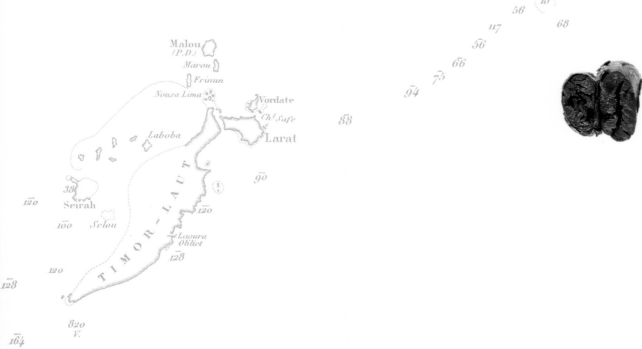

Qualities

Eating a square of fine chocolate unleashes a series of sensations, from the initial unfurling of flavor to the depth of the long notes that remain on the palate once the chocolate has melted away to nothing. Cacao itself is bitter, but the edge is usually taken off by adding sugar or honey. Other flavors can also be added, such as milk, almond, barley, aniseed, cinnamon, vanilla, and chili pepper—as the Aztecs did.

It is rare to find people who dislike chocolate. Many people actively crave it and find it enhances their moods.

Uses

The Mayans and Aztecs drank cacao as a refreshing and nourishing drink. The Spanish conquistadors preferred it warm and with added sugar.

During the eighteenth century, bars of chocolate were available but were considered a real luxury.

Non-sweetened cacao is still widely used as a spice in Central and South America, in recipes such as the famous Mexican sauce "el mole," a spicy sauce made with chilies and chocolate that is eaten with turkey or other meats.

I think cacao is a remarkable spice, and I particularly like playing with its bitterness. I remember when I was still a novice chef producing a duck in chocolate sauce that a number of my friends still talk about. However, as a spice, cacao needs to be used carefully to bring out its finer qualities.

The finest chocolates

Unfortunately, these days, it is becoming increasingly difficult to find chocolate-makers who produce their wares directly from the whole beans. This is a pity, for such chocolates can be compared to the finest champagnes, each with its own characteristic taste. I recommend chuao from Venezuela for its slightly acid yet smooth notes, Madagascar beans for their intensity, and Sri Lankan beans for their fruity taste. Fine chocolate should not be too dark in color. Look out for chocolate with a mahogany sheen. For milk chocolate, Java beans, with their slightly caramel taste, are ideal.

Cacao from Ecuador generally has a slightly fermented taste. The beans from Jamaica are delicate in flavor with an elegant note of hazelnut, and those from Grenada are fruity with just a hint of spicy freshness.

Health benefits

When cacao first arrived in Europe, some doctors warned their patients off it, believing it to be poisonous. However, it soon came to be seen as nourishing, easily digested, and energy-giving, and was even considered an aphrodisiac. Cacao was never more popular than in eighteenth-century Europe. Its reputation as an aphrodisiac—which the Aztecs were well aware of—meant that it was prized by aristocratic libertines, who served hot chocolate in elegant and precious receptacles.

Cacao is very rich in vitamin D. It contains theobromine, which is a stimulant yet has a soothing effect on the nerves.

Setting the Course—The time is as ripe now for celebrating the rich union of the cocoa bean and the chili pepper as it was for the ancient Maya. In my search for this lush and fiery combination, I have pinned it down to another time and place: the dining rooms of the finer households of Saint-Malo in the nineteenth century. Even then these flavors were valued, softened with the distinguished, sweet tones of lobster trapped in salted butter and sherry. Today, this combination is coming back into fashion. We add the freshness of lemon zest and green mango.

Nineteenth-Century-Style Lobster

Crew of 4

Rigging
Strainer
Hammer
Medium-holed grater
Small handheld blender
4 soup plates

Cruising Time
3 hours

From the Ship's Hold
Puligny-Montrachet, Meursault or Château Chalon

Provisions

Galley Pantry 1
4 Breton lobsters, 1 lb. (500 g) each
5 tbs (75 g) + 2 tbs (25 g) + 3 tbs (35 g) salted butter

Galley Pantry 2
Sauce Base
½ cup (10 cl) Amontillado Sherry
¼ vanilla bean (pod)
10 annatto seeds
1 tsp coriander seeds
Dash of bitter cocoa powder
4 sprigs chervil
2 cups (50 cl) chicken bouillon
½ cup (12 cl) water
2 tbs sherry vinegar
½ lemon

March 15, 2003. Southwesterly breeze, force 4 to 5. Sky heavy with clouds; sea rough.

First Tack

At least two hours before the meal, scald the lobsters in boiling water for 4 minutes. Separate the heads and claws from the bodies. Shell the claws and tails. Cut the tails in half along their length, remove the gut and recover as much coral as possible. Set aside.

Second Tack

Sauce base (Galley Pantry 2): Split the heads in two and remove the sand pouches. Crush the heads with the hammer. Sauté the shells in 5 tbs (75 g) salted butter (Galley Pantry 1), then add the sherry and bring to a vigorous boil. Add the vanilla bean cut into slivers, the annatto seeds, coriander seeds, bitter cocoa, and chervil. Add the bouillon and the water and cook gently for 45 minutes, by which time the volume should have reduced by one-third. Strain, pressing out as much liquid as possible.

Third Tack

Garnish (Galley Pantry 3): Peel the green mango and grate it to a medium coarseness. Set aside.

Landfall

Five to 10 minutes before serving, melt 2 tbs (25 g) salted butter (Galley Pantry 1) in a pan and sear the tail pieces and claws. Place in a dish, cover with damp paper towel to prevent drying out, and keep warm in the oven at 200°F (100°C). Deglaze the pan with sherry vinegar (Galley Pantry 2), bring to boil, add the sauce base and reduce by at least one-third. Add the remaining 3 tbs (35 g) butter (Galley Pantry 1) and the reserved coral. Once the butter and coral are well mixed in, the resulting sauce should have a slightly syrupy consistency. Add the juice of half a lemon (Galley Pantry 2). Strain and liquidize. Warm 4 large soup plates. Lay a fine line of cocoa powder on the edge of each plate, and a parallel line of green mango. Place the lobster tails in the center of the plate and arrange the claws parallel with the lines of mango and cocoa. Cover the claws and tails generously with sauce and finely grate one quarter of a lemon over the plate. Transfer the rest of the sauce into a sauceboat. Serve.

with Sherry and Cocoa

Galley Pantry 3
Garnish
1 large green mango

Finishing
1 whole lemon
A little bitter cocoa

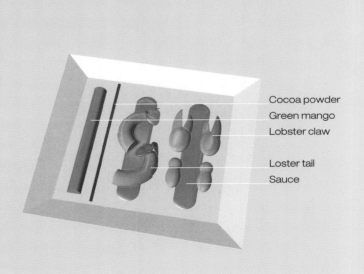

Cocoa powder
Green mango
Lobster claw

Loster tail
Sauce

Setting the Course—In the Orient the relationship between mint and coriander is a tender and ancient love affair. But I like to play the matchmaker, and see what comes of new couplings. Mint, I thought, really should introduce the demure coriander to his powerful friend, chocolate. But, since the rich and influential are often quick to judge a stranger, perhaps it would be better to veil the newcomer's identity, leaving her a fair chance of being appreciated on her own merits. Enter caramel, a chaperone, to mediate in this delightful meeting between the Orient and the New World.

After Dinner: Mint and Chocolate

Crew of 4

Rigging
Sorbet maker
Nonstick baking sheet
Flexible spatula
Pastry bag with plain tip ½ in.
   (1 cm) in diameter
Small handheld blender
Wax paper
Cooking thermometer
4 plates

Cruising Time
24 hours

From the Ship's Hold
Vintage Maury

Provisions

Galley Pantry 1
Chocolate Macaroons
9 tbs chopped almonds
12 tbs sifted confectioner's sugar
2 tbs cocoa powder
5 tbs egg whites
2 tbs sugar

Galley Pantry 2
Coriander Ganache
½ cup (100 g) cream
1 tsp glucose
1 oz. (25 g) fresh coriander
4½ oz. (125 g) covering chocolate
   (70% cocoa solids)
1½ tbs (25 g) butter

Galley Pantry 3
Mint Ganache
½ cup (100 g) cream
1 tsp glucose
1 oz. (25 g) fresh mint
4½ oz. (125 g) covering chocolate
   (70% cocoa solids)
1½ tbs (25 g) butter

Galley Pantry 4
Caramel Sauce
9 tbs sugar
6 tbs cream
4 tbs (60 g) butter

October 9, 2003. Wind southwesterly, force 6 gusting 7. Sea getting very rough, squalls.

First Tack

Chocolate macaroons (Galley Pantry 1): Using the handheld blender, grind the almonds, confectioner's sugar, and cocoa to a fine powder. Sift onto the baking sheet and leave to dry out for 24 hours. Whisk the egg whites to stiff peaks. Fold in the sugar a little at a time until completely smooth. Using the spatula, gradually fold in the almond, sugar, and cocoa powder. Fill the pastry bag and pipe straight ribbons onto the nonstick baking sheet, as with choux pastry. If the mixture is too dry, add a little unbeaten egg white. No peaks should be visible. Leave the macaroons to dry until a film forms on the surface. Preheat oven to 300°F (150°C) and bake for 5 minutes. To remove the macaroons from the baking sheet more easily, pour a little water under the wax paper. Turn over and set aside on wax paper.

Second Tack

Coriander ganache (Galley Pantry 2): Place the cream and glucose in a small pan and bring to boil. Add the coriander, liquidize with the handheld blender and leave to infuse for 15 minutes. Filter through strainer, pressing well. Melt the butter and chocolate together in a double boiler. Combine the two mixtures.

Third Tack

Mint ganache (Galley Pantry 3): Place the cream and glucose in a small pan and bring to boil. Add the mint, liquidize with the handheld blender and leave to infuse for 15 minutes. Filter through strainer, pressing well. Melt the butter and chocolate together in a double boiler. Combine the two mixtures.

Fourth Tack

Caramel sauce (Galley Pantry 4): Place the sugar in an ungreased pan and caramelize until golden brown. Incorporate the cream a little at a time. Return pan to heat and add the butter. Stir well for a few minutes. Set aside.

Fifth Tack

Chocolate sauce (Galley Pantry 5): Chop the chocolate finely and place in a bowl. Heat the 6 tbs cream and pour onto the chocolate. Make a syrup with the water and sugar; add the cocoa, then the 3 tbs cream. Combine the two mixtures and whisk while heating to boiling point. Set aside.

Sixth Tack

Mint chocolate ice cream (Galley Pantry 6): Place the milk, powdered milk, and sugar in a double boiler and heat to 180°F (82°C). Cool the mixture by placing the bowl in ice. When cold, add the mint extract. Pour into sorbet-maker and start, adding the chopped chocolate once it is in motion.

Landfall

Prepare four large square plates. Pour a line of chocolate sauce and a line of caramel sauce along the left side of each plate. Coat 3 macaroons with both coriander and mint ganache. Stand the macaroons upright, sticking them in place with a little ganache. Place a scoop of ice cream next to each macaroon. Serve.

Galley Pantry 5
Chocolate Sauce

2 oz. (60 g) covering chocolate (70% cocoa solids)
6 + 3 tbs cream
½ cup (10 cl) water
6 tbs sugar
4 tbs cocoa powder

Galley Pantry 6
Mint Chocolate Ice Cream

¾ cup (200 g) milk
5 tbs powdered milk
4 tbs sugar
2 tbs mint extract (available at groceries)
4 tbs coarsely chopped chocolate (70% cocoa solids)

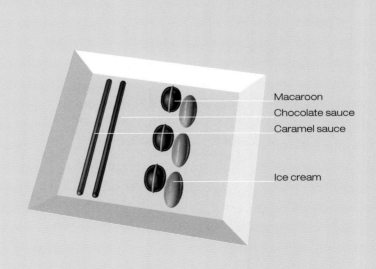

Macaroon
Chocolate sauce
Caramel sauce

Ice cream

Setting the Course—Coffee contrasts as powerfully with chocolate as hot does with cold. But in this composition they are subdued by the full tenderness and delicacy of the flavor of India—the curry leaf. Its aroma is like a combination of mandarin orange and toast. For me, it is absolutely synonymous with the cuisine of Mauritius.

Contrast and Harmony: Coffee, Cho

Crew of 4

Rigging
Sorbet maker
Small handheld blender
Strainer
Large-holed grater
Nonstick baking tray
4 stainless-steel rings, ½ in. (1.5 cm) high,
   3½ in. (9.5 cm) across
Airtight container
4 coffee cups
4 plates

Cruising Time
5 hours

From the Ship's Hold
Rivesaltes sur Grains

Provisions

Galley Pantry 1
Cocoa Pastry for Tartlets
2⅓ cups (225 g) flour
4 tbs cocoa
1 tbs (10 g) baking powder
½ cup (125 g) butter
¾ cup (100 g) sifted confectioner's sugar
1 egg

Galley Pantry 2
Filling for Tartlets
2½ oz. (75 g) dark chocolate (70% cocoa solids)
3 tbs (45 g) butter
4 egg yolks and 4 egg whites
3½ tbs sugar
2 tbs (15 g) cocoa powder

October 22, 2003. Fresh southeasterly wind, force 4 to 5. Rough sea; low visibility.

First Tack

Cocoa pastry for tartlets (Galley Pantry 1): Work the flour, cocoa, baking powder, butter, and confectioner's sugar between the fingers. Mix in the egg. Set aside, covered. When the dough has hardened, butter the pastry rings and place on the baking tray. Divide the dough in halves. Press one half into the pastry rings to a thickness of ½ in. (1.5 mm). Refrigerate for 15 minutes. Cover the tartlet cases with aluminum foil to protect the edges and blind bake for 8 minutes at 325°F (170°C). Remove the foil and set aside. Grate the rest of the dough onto a baking sheet with the cheese grater and bake the shavings in the oven for 5 minutes at 325°F (170°C). Cool.

Second Tack

Filling for tartlets (Galley Pantry 2): Melt the chocolate and butter together in a double boiler. Whisk the egg whites to stiff peaks. Pour in the sugar. Beat the egg yolks and add them. Delicately fold in the sifted cocoa, then the melted chocolate and butter. Fill the tartlet bases with the resulting cream. Sprinkle the crust shavings on top.

Third Tack

Curry-leaf ice cream (Galley Pantry 3): Bring to boil the milk, cream, and 2 tbs sugar. Whisk the egg yolks with the other 2 tbs sugar for 5 minutes. Pour on the boiling milk. Chop the curry leaves finely with the handheld blender, and add them to the mixture. Allow to infuse until cool, then strain and pour into the sorbet maker.

Fourth Tack

Coffee granita (Galley Pantry 4): Add the sugar to the coffee and place in the freezer. After 4 hours, scrape off flakes of frozen coffee with a fork into an airtight container. Return to the freezer.

Fifth Tack

Whipped cream (Galley Pantry 5): Whisk the cream and confectioner's sugar together until light and fluffy. Refrigerate.

Sixth Tack

Chocolate sauce (Galley Pantry 6): Place the cocoa, milk, and sugar in a pan. Bring to boil and allow to cool. Refrigerate.

Landfall

Prepare four large square plates. On the left, draw two lines of chocolate sauce. Place the tartlet in the middle. Fill the coffee cups half with curry leaf ice cream, half with coffee granita. Add a spoonful of whipped cream on the top. Sprinkle with cocoa powder. Place the coffee cup at the top right of the plate. Serve.

:olate, Curry

Galley Pantry 3
Curry-Leaf Ice Cream
½ cup (12.5 cl) milk
½ cup (125 g) cream
2 + 2 tbs sugar
3 egg yolks
3 tsp dried curry leaves

Galley Pantry 4
Coffee Granita
½ cup (125 g) strong espresso coffee
3 tbs confectioner's sugar

Galley Pantry 5
Whipped Cream
½ cup (125 g) cream
2 tsp confectioner's sugar

Galley Pantry 6
Chocolate Sauce
½ cup (125 g) milk
4 tsp cocoa powder
4 tsp sugar

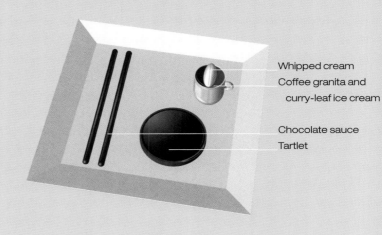

Whipped cream
Coffee granita and
    curry-leaf ice cream

Chocolate sauce
Tartlet

Setting the Course—I am particularly fond of those stories one hears round the fire while the storm rages outside. The passionate epic of the cocoa bean could be one such story: its memorable encounters, its love stories, its betrayals. I have made up this spicy adventure in its honor, on the theme of the traditional cup of hot chocolate.

First Tack
Bring the milk to boil with the spices and leave to infuse for 30 minutes. Chop the chocolate fairly finely and place in a saucepan. Strain the milk onto the chocolate. Stir until smooth and creamy.

Landfall
Reheat without boiling, whisk up a froth on top, and serve.

Spicy Hot Chocolate

Crew of 4

Rigging
Strainer

Cruising Time
45 minutes

Provisions

Galley Pantry 1
Chocolate
Ideally, use high-quality covering
   chocolate
3 cups (75 cl) milk
3½ oz. (100 g) chocolate
   (70% cocoa solids)

Galley Pantry 2
Spices
⅓ nutmeg
½ cinnamon stick
2 star anise
1 peppercorn
½ vanilla bean (pod), split
   lengthwise

January 10, 2001. Near gale warning. Northwesterly force 6 to 7, occasionally gale 8. Sea rough. Visibility reduced to 1 or 2 miles in squalls. Temperatures near freezing.

Sugar cane:
Sweetness in the wild
latitude 10°45'0" N, longitude 106°40'0" E

India and Cochin China. This pretty plant has journeyed halfway around the world, much to the delight of those with a sweet tooth. It probably first grew in the wild in India and Cochin China.

History

This pretty plant has journeyed halfway around the world, much to the delight of those with a sweet tooth. It probably first grew in the wild in India and Cochin China. The Chinese were harvesting and refining sugar cane by 200 B.C.E. at the latest. At the same time, the Hebrews had no knowledge of the plant, and the Greeks were barely aware of its existence. Only in the early years of the first century C.E. did sugar cane reach Rome.

The Arabs discovered the plant in India and introduced it to Egypt, Spain, Sicily, Madeira, and the Canaries.

The Crusaders brought the sugar back to Europe, where it quickly became a much-sought-after luxury.

In 1493, Christopher Columbus planted the first sugar cane in Hispaniola—the name he gave to what is now Haiti. A few years later, in 1497, the Portuguese finally managed to sail around the Cape of Good Hope, thereby making the old maritime trading routes redundant. Lisbon took over from Venice and Genoa as the main point of entry into Europe for imported cargo. The Portuguese capital also became the principal center for refining sugar imported from the Orient.

During the course of the sixteenth century, sugar cane spread throughout the Caribbean, from Puerto Rico and Cuba to Jamaica. Cortez and the Spanish planted the cane in Mexico and Peru, while the Portuguese introduced it to Brazil. By the early eighteenth century, the English and French held vast plantations in their colonies in the Caribbean. These labor-intensive plantations led to the tragedy of a flourishing slave trade. The European and American love of sugar has led to a vast global sugar industry. Most sugar refineries were based in the great ports.

In the late eighteenth and early nineteenth centuries, sugar became scarce as a result of political turmoil in Europe which led to embargoes and restrictions on imports. Napoleon encouraged farmers to come up with a method of extracting sugar from sugar beet. The process proved easier than expected and, for the first time, the monopoly on sugar from the Caribbean was broken. The dispute over the two sources of sugar lasted for decades. When slavery was abolished in the mid-nineteenth century, the yield from the plantations in the West Indies dwindled.

In the late nineteenth century, sugar production far outstripped consumption. Sugar producers played a part in the development of advertising as they tried to increase demand and thus sell off their excess stock. This may explain the extremely high sugar content of many recipes dating from the period—and indeed today.

In the twentieth century, sugar beet production slowed during the two world wars, which meant that sugar cane production rose as a result. Today, people generally eat far too much sugar. I find a little sugar goes a long way.

Natural history
Sugar cane, *Saccharum officinarum*, is a member of the grass family. The canes, which resemble giant reeds, can grow to a height of six to fifteen feet (2–5 m).

Qualities
Scientists have shown that even newborn babies like the taste of sugar. Before sugar cane reached the West, the only natural sources of sweetening were honey and fruits.

Uses
All Western societies consume far too much sugar. This is one of the principal causes of the obesity epidemic that is currently developing, bringing a host of other diseases such as diabetes in its wake. I always cut the amount of sugar suggested in recipes for cakes and biscuits by at least a third. Preventing children from eating candy bars rich in saturated fats and drinking sugary sodas would lead to a great improvement in the overall health of the nation.

I do use sugar, of course, but in unexpected ways, to bring out the flavor of savory dishes. A pinch of sugar is marvelous in a simple vinaigrette, for example. The sweetness counterbalances the salty or acidic taste of some ingredients. This is important in many sauces, particularly those served with fish and seafood in general, which are often rather acidic. Sugar will never entirely mask bitterness, however much is used.

The finest sugars
It used to be the case that the finest sugar was Egyptian. These days, sugar cane is grown in both the northern and southern hemispheres, between 35° north and 30° south. It needs a warm, wet climate. Sugar cane has the highest sugar content when it is grown at a low altitude near the sea. Some of the finest sugar comes from Mauritius, where the green expanses of the plantations by the edge of the Indian Ocean are a striking sight.

The best unrefined sugars are named according to their granulometry and how unrefined they are—golden granulated, golden caster, and fine golden caster. These sugars have a delicate taste of honey and are perfect for baking cakes and biscuits. I like to add a spoonful of dry, standard, or fine demerara to yogurt, pancakes, and tea. The powerful taste of brown or light brown muscovado sugar, reminiscent of spices, pineapple, and licorice, reminds me of balsamic vinegar. Treacly, sticky sugar, dark or light brown in color, it has a powerful, heady aroma of rum and peppery licorice. It is perfect for cocktails with a kick such as ti'punch.

Sugar comes in a wide variety of flavors. It is a shame always to stick to refined white sugar.

Health benefits
All I can say is: to be used in moderation!

Setting the Course—At the high tides of the autumn equinox, the time comes to press the new cider. Space is needed in the cellars. So any cider left over from the previous year is boiled up with the pulp of the newly pressed apples, along with any barrel-ends that have turned to vinegar. A syrupy, sweet, aromatic vinegar is the result, very much like an apple balsamic. Then the sea bass, white as the crest of a wave, rolls in from the coast to the orchards, sent by the swell all along the cliffs of the north of Brittany.

Strips of Sea Bass with Celtic Vinegar

180

Crew of 4

Rigging
Wax paper
Salmon slicer
Strainer
Small handheld blender
4 plates

Cruising Time
2 hours

From the Ship's Hold
Coteaux de l'Aubance

Provisions

Galley Pantry 1
1 line-caught sea bass weighing 2 lb. (1 kg)
Fleur de sel
Freshly-ground salt and white pepper

Galley Pantry 2
Marinade for Bass
8 tbs grape-seed oil
1 tsp hazelnut oil
3 tbs sherry vinegar

October 28, 2001. Strong southwesterly breeze, force 5 gusting 6, squally showers.

First Tack

Marinade (Galley Pantry 2): Whisk the grape-seed oil, hazelnut oil, and sherry vinegar together, season with salt and pepper. Set aside.

Second Tack

Prepare the strips of sea bass (Galley Pantry 1): Fillet the fish, remove the skin and bones. Use the salmon slicer to cut the fillets along their length, then lay them flat on a sheet of wax paper and cut into strips ½ in. (1.5 cm) wide.

Landfall

Place the strips of bass in a dish. Emulsify the marinade again and pour it on the fish. Leave for 5 minutes. Lay the strips out on a large, flat, cool plate, in parallel lines with ⅛ in. (3 mm) between each line, filling the plate. Drizzle Celtic or balsamic vinegar (Galley Pantry 3) into the spaces. Grind a little white pepper over the dish and sprinkle on a few grains of fleur de sel. Serve with toasted slices of rustic French bread.

Galley Pantry 3
Celtic Vinegar

This vinegar is available ready to use at Les Maisons de Bricourt (see Vinaigre Celtique, page 234) and in some groceries. A possible replacement is a very high-quality balsamic vinegar.

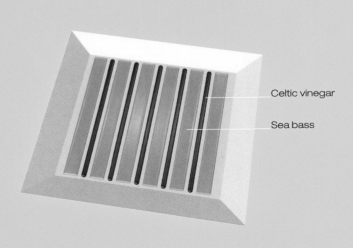

Celtic vinegar

Sea bass

Setting the Course—The pearly white flesh of the turbot, the "king of the seas," nestles cozily under a crunchy shell of seeds and almonds, delicately perfumed by a subtle scent from across the Indian Ocean: the curry leaf. The baby bean sprouts have a vitality I find adorable. This is perhaps their first meeting with citrus fruits and vegetables.

First Tack

Curry-leaf oil (Galley Pantry 3): Put the crushed curry leaves and the grape-seed oil in one of the Mason jars, close tightly and sterilize in a boiling-water bath for 10 minutes counting from second boil. Set aside until the day of the meal.

Lemon syrup: Cut one of the lemons into quarters and chop coarsely. Place in the second Mason jar. In a small pan, bring to the boil the 3 tbs sugar, 3 tbs water, and the juice of the second lemon. Boil well for 3 minutes and pour into the jar. Close the jar, making sure the seal is airtight. Set aside until the day of the meal.

Grapefruit conserve: Using the vegetable peeler, remove a band of peel about ½ in. (1 cm) wide, all around the grapefruit. Chop the peel, place in a pan of cold water, bring to the boil and drain. Completely peel the grapefruit and separate the segments, being careful not to leave any white skin. In a small pan, place the grapefruit peel, grapefruit segments, and the 4 tbs sugar. Simmer gently together until the peel becomes transparent. Set aside.

Turbot with Poppy Seeds and Sesame

182

Crew of 4

Rigging
Vegetable peeler
2 Mason jars
Fine-holed grater
Plastic wrap
Japanese mandolin
Mortar and pestle
Baking dish 8 x 10 in. (20 x 30 cm)
4 plates

Cruising Time
48 hours

From the Ship's Hold
White Hermitage

Provisions

Galley Pantry 1
1 whole turbot weighing 4½ lb. (2 kg). Ask your fish seller
   to fillet and skin it for you.
Fleur de sel
Freshly-ground salt and white pepper

Galley Pantry 2
Garnish
2 medium zucchini
1 clove garlic
1 cup (100 g) soy or mung bean sprouts
1 tbs olive oil
1 lemon

Galley Pantry 3
Curry-Leaf Oil
½ cup (12 cl) grape-seed oil
25 small curry leaves

March 15, 2000. Gentle breeze from the northwest, force 3 to 4. Slight swell.

Second Tack

Crust (Galley Pantry 4): Prepare the day before. Toast the sesame and linseeds in a pan. Lightly roast the hazelnuts and almonds in a hot oven in separate containers until light golden brown. Cool. Crush the hazelnuts, almonds and pistachios separately with the mortar and pestle. In a small pan, heat the salted butter until just melted, and add the sesame, poppy seeds, linseeds, almonds, pistachios, and hazelnuts. Line the baking dish with a perfectly smooth layer of plastic wrap, avoiding any folds. Pour in the mixture and flatten to a uniform thickness. Refrigerate until the next day.

Third Tack

On the day of the meal, finish the lemon syrup. Recover all the juice in the jar (see First Tack) and strain it, pressing out as much as possible. Reduce this juice by half. Refrigerate. The syrup should thicken. Filter the curry leaf oil and set aside. Prepare the turbot (Galley Pantry 1). Cut the fillets into 4 equal portions. Refrigerate.

Fourth Tack

Prepare the garnish (Galley Pantry 2). Julienne the zucchini: wash them well, dry if necessary, top and tail, then cut into four chunks. Use the mandolin to cut three very thin slices from the side of one piece. Give the chunk a quarter turn and cut another three slivers. Repeat the process 4 times for each piece. The heart of the zucchini is not used in this recipe. Slice each little pile of three slivers lengthwise to obtain fine strings. Set aside. Peel the garlic clove and stick it on the end of a fork.

Landfall

Preheat the oven to 325°F (170°C). Season the pieces of fish with freshly-ground salt and pepper. Turn out the solidified crust and carefully remove the plastic wrap. Place the fish in the baking dish. Cut the butter crust into pieces to cover the turbot fillets as carefully as possible. Bake for 14 minutes. Meanwhile, reheat the grapefruit conserve. Preheat the olive oil in a frying pan to a high heat, and toss the julienned zucchini and the bean sprouts using the garlic-tipped fork. Keep turning to avoid coloring. Grate in a little lemon zest and season. Lay out a line of grapefruit conserve one third of the way across the plate. Place a portion of turbot in the center, and add the zucchini and bean sprouts, placing them between the grapefruit conserve and the edge. On the remaining two-thirds of the plate, pour 3 tsp lemon syrup and 4 tsp curry leaf oil. Grate a little lemon zest over the plate and place a few fleur de sel crystals on the turbot. Serve.

with a Grapefruit Conserve

Lemon Syrup
2 lemons
3 tbs sugar
3 tbs water

Grapefruit Conserve
1 grapefruit
4 tbs sugar

Galley Pantry 4
Crust
4 tbs (50 g) salted butter
2 tsp sesame seeds, toasted
1 tsp linseeds, toasted
10 hazelnuts, lightly roasted
10 blanched almonds, lightly roasted
1 tsp poppy seeds
1 tsp pistachio kernels

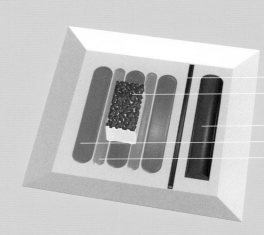

Grapefruit conserve
Turbot

Zucchini and bean sprouts
Curry-leaf oil
Lemon syrup

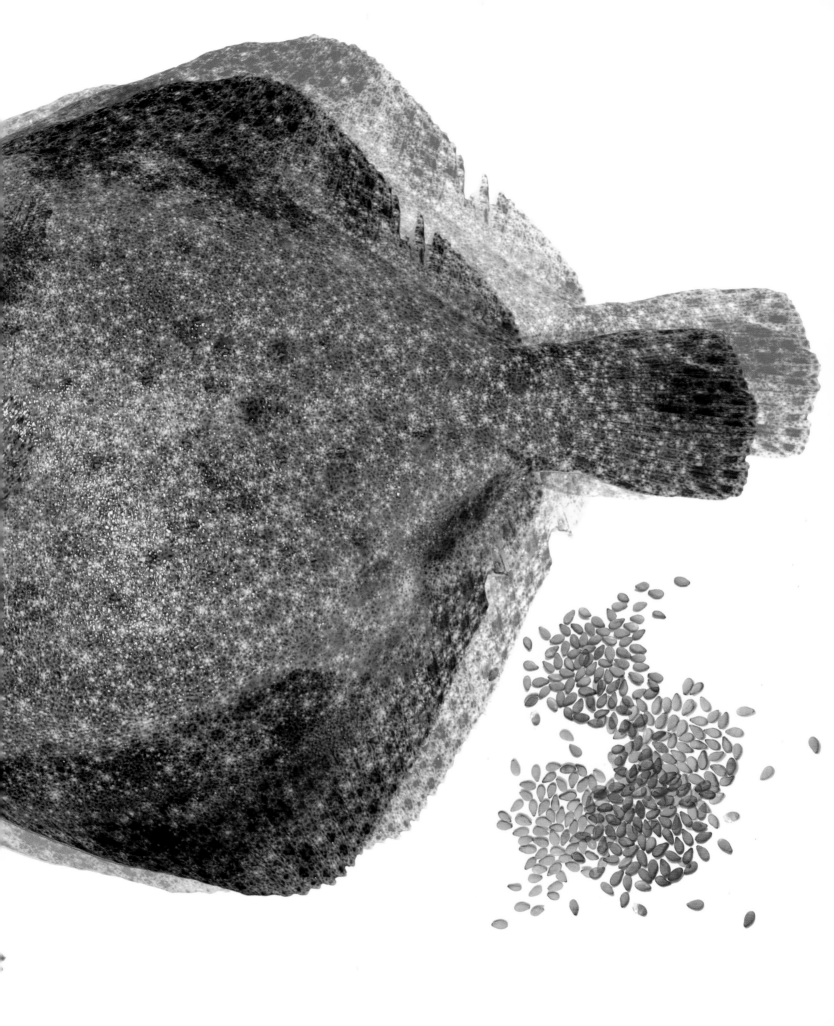

Setting the Course—We are out at sea in the Caribbean one morning, approaching the island of Grenada. Suddenly, a powerful fragrance envelops us: a blend of nutmeg, mace, and cloves, floating in the air, mingling with the sultry mugginess of the coast and the salty taste of the trade winds. This composition, dedicated to the little lobsters caught by Philippe Couapel, is an attempt to recreate that wonderful feeling and complex flavor.

Small Lobster with the Flavors of the

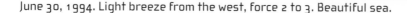

Crew of 4

Rigging
Hammer
Large knife for halving lobsters
Strainer
Plastic wrap
Small handheld blender
4 plates

Cruising Time
4 hours

From the Ship's Hold
Alsace Pinot Gris or Condrieu

Provisions

Galley Pantry 1
2 Brittany lobsters weighing 1 ½ lb. (800 g) each
6 live velvet swimming crabs

Galley Pantry 2
First Base
3½ oz. (100 g) fresh ginger
3½ oz. (100 g) fresh galingale
2 tbs sunflower oil
½ vanilla bean (pod)
1 stick lemon grass, fresh if possible
   (available at Asian groceries)
1 nutmeg
2 cloves garlic
10 Jamaican peppercorns
1 heaped tsp (10 g) tamarind paste
   (available at Asian groceries)
4 cups (1 liter) chicken bouillon

June 30, 1994. Light breeze from the west, force 2 to 3. Beautiful sea.

First Tack

First base (Galley Pantry 2): Peel and chop the ginger and the galingale and sweat them in a pan in the sunflower oil. Add the vanilla and chopped lemon grass. Crush the nutmeg with the hammer and add it to the pan. Add the garlic whole, with the peppercorns and tamarind paste. Stir regularly until the tamarind has mixed in well. Add the chicken bouillon and simmer very gently for 1½ hours.

Second Tack

Fig rolls (Galley Pantry 4): Chop the figs and dates. Add the dash of five spice and the juice of the quarter lemon. Mix well. Lay out a square of plastic wrap. Spoon the mixture into a sausage shape in the middle of the wrap. Fold the wrap over and seal the ends. Roll the sausage by its ends, which will tighten the mixture and give it a round shape. Place in the freezer for at least 2 hours to firm up for slicing. Sharp muscovado dressing (Galley Pantry 4): Dissolve the muscovado sugar in the sherry vinegar. Set aside in a small pot.

Third Tack

Second base (Galley Pantry 3): Strain the first base, pressing out as much liquid as possible. Crush the velvet swimming crabs (Galley Pantry 1) with the hammer.

Sauté them in the unsalted butter. Add the annatto seeds, the Thai basil, and the dash of Cayenne pepper. Add the liquid from the first base. Cook evenly for one hour then strain, pressing hard. Set aside. Take the fig roll out of the freezer and cut into four cylindrical pieces. Set aside.

Landfall

A quarter of an hour before the meal, scald the lobsters in boiling water for 6 minutes. Cut them in halves, separate the heads, the claws and the bodies. Remove the sand pouches from the heads. Spread each half head with 2 tbs salted butter and put them under a hot grill for ten minutes. Shell the claws and tails. Reheat the sauce without letting it boil and whisk in the remaining unsalted butter. Warm four large plates. Arrange a half-head, a half-body, and 1 claw on each plate. On one side place the fig roll, and on the other a line of muscovado dressing. Blend the sauce until it forms an emulsion and pour generously onto the lobster meat. Serve.

Spice Islands

Galley Pantry 3
Second Base
1½ tbs (20 g) unsalted butter
1½ oz. (50 g) Thai basil
1 tsp annatto seeds
Dash of Cayenne pepper

Finishing
2 tbs (30 g) salted butter + 2 tbs (30 g) unsalted butter

Galley Pantry 4
Fig Rolls
5 dried figs
2 dates
Dash of Chinese five spice
¼ lemon

Sharp Muscovado Dressing
1 tbsp. muscovado sugar
2 tbs sherry vinegar

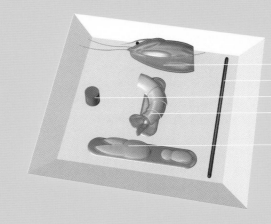

Lobster half-head
Muscovado dressing
Fig roll
Lobster half-body and sauce
Lobster claw and sauce

Vanilla:
The taste of tenderness
latitude 4°52'60" S, longitude 47°12'0" W

South America. The first European to encounter vanilla was Christopher Columbus, who was introduced to the spice by the Aztecs, whose princes drank it mixed with cacao and chili pepper on special occasions.

History

The first European to encounter vanilla was Christopher Columbus, who was introduced to the spice by the Aztecs, whose princes drank it mixed with cacao and chili pepper on special occasions. It quickly became very popular in Spain and spread to France in 1664. Louis XV grew vanilla orchids in his greenhouses in the mid-eighteenth century. In Mexico, the orchid was naturally fertilized by the melipone bee, which meant that the Mexicans were able to monopolize production until 1841, when the problem of how to fertilize the plant artificially was finally solved. Some people claim that the mystery was solved by the Belgian naturalist Charles Morren, while others believe the discovery was made by a nameless slave in La Réunion. Once the process of artificial pollination was understood, the orchids could be transplanted elsewhere. They were soon flourishing in Tahiti, Madagascar, Mauritius, La Réunion, and in the Comoro islands.

Today, vanilla is widely used in desserts throughout the world. However, in 90 percent of cases, the vanilla aroma is obtained from a chemical named methylprotocatechuic aldehyde.

Natural history

Vanilla planifolia or *V. fragrans* is not, as is often thought, a pod or a bean, but rather the dried fruit of a liana of the orchid family. It is harvested before it ripens, soaked in warm water, then dried and left to ferment for nearly two months. During this fermentation process, the plant's natural enzymes produce a number of complex compounds, including heliotropin, vanillin, and alcohol. The fruits are then left to dry in the sun or in special ovens until they turn shiny, black, oily, wrinkled, and sometimes covered in crystals because they sweat benzoic acid.

It is a long, complicated process, and because a certain proportion of the fruits rot, the price of true vanilla is inevitably high. In terms of price per ounce, vanilla is the second most costly spice after saffron.

Qualities

The smooth, sweet flavor of vanilla, with a light overtone of tobacco, is one of the most delicious of all spices. Artificial vanilla is heavy, slightly acrid, and the taste is less long-lasting.

Natural vanilla is the real taste of childhood for many people.

Uses

Vanilla is one of my favorite spices. It has been used since the seventeenth century in conjunction with chocolate and coffee, and it also goes well with milk-based recipes, creams, yogurts, and ice creams. It also heightens the taste of many fruits. I like adding a touch of vanilla to nage sauces for crayfish and lobster. I also use it

in a number of fish recipes, but it needs to be used with care as it can easily overpower other ingredients. Even so, I find that its warm, smooth aroma often rounds off a dish wonderfully.

One of the finest marriages is between vanilla and almond—in almond paste, for example. It also goes marvelously well with ginger, pineapple, rhubarb, and dark chocolate.

Since vanilla is so expensive, I try and extract every last drop of flavor from each bean. To begin with, I store my beans in a sealed container of sugar, which takes on the flavor. If I want to use vanilla in a sauce, I cut off a small section about an inch in length, which I then split in two so I can scrape the inside of the pod with the blade of a knife. Once the sauce is ready, I rinse and dry the pod and put it back in the sealed container.

The finest vanilla

The finest natural vanilla comes from Veracruz in Mexico. Most natural vanilla comes from Madagascar, although it is not necessarily of the highest quality because of the cyclones that frequently disrupt the harvest, and because a number of farmers pick the fruit too early in order to reach the market sooner.

La Réunion is often considered to have the finest regular production, although much of the harvest of Bourbon vanilla, which is generally thought to come from La Réunion, in fact comes from Madagascar.

In Tahiti a variety known as Vanilla pompona is grown. This produces shorter, thicker fruit which are often more oily than other varieties. This variety has a particularly delicate aroma and is often used in perfume.

Health benefits

Vanilla can be used to treat chronic bronchitis and smokers' coughs. It is tonic, stimulant, and antiseptic, and also aids digestion.

It was once believed that vanilla was a cure for melancholy. There may be some truth in this, and I can certainly recommend it as a comfort food. I like to serve vanilla desserts to serious businessmen to watch them rediscover the tastes of their childhood.

Setting the Course—There is a whiteness that is characteristic of Brittany, in its shellfish and in its vegetables. Here they are combined in the warm, sweet intensity of the bewitching vanilla bean. The white florets of the cauliflower—which squeak satisfyingly when you cut them—are indistinguishable from coral. It is grown everywhere in the Saint-Malo area, where the sea spray comes in to envelop the bulbous white heads. Nothing could be healthier than a light, white cauliflower cream for these sweet, white little scallops. The combination is heightened by the tropical nut.

Queen Scallops with Vanilla Cauliflowe

Crew of 4

Rigging
Strainer
Small handheld blender
Mason jar
Nutmeg grater
4 soup plates

Cruising Time
24 hours

From the Ship's Hold
Vouvray demi-sec or a Montlouis demi-sec

Provisions

Galley Pantry 1
2 lbs. (1 kg) queen scallops, in their shells

Galley Pantry 2
Cauliflower Cream
1 whole cauliflower weighing about 2 lbs. (1 kg)
4 cups (1 liter) water
2 cups (50 cl) milk
1 tsp salt
Grated nutmeg
1 small bird pepper
1 tsp Espelette pepper powder

October 18, 2003. Wind from the southwest, force 4 to 5. Rain severely reducing visibility.

First Tack

Vanilla Oil (Galley Pantry 3): Slit the vanilla beans open lengthwise and put them into the Mason jar with the grape-seed oil. Close tightly and sterilize in boiling water for 10 minutes. Allow to cool in sterilizing bath until next day.

Second Tack

On the day of the meal, shell the scallops (Galley Pantry 1). Wash under cold running water but do not soak. Dry on paper towel and set aside in a strainer.

Third Tack

One hour before the meal, prepare the cauliflower cream (Galley Pantry 2). Trim off and divide the cauliflower florets. Cut each floret into 4 pieces. Place the water, milk, salt, grated nutmeg, and cauliflower pieces in a pan. Bring to the boil, simmer gently for 10 minutes, remove from heat. Split open the bird pepper and discard the seeds; add to the pan and leave to infuse. After 10 minutes, remove the pepper and strain, pressing through as much pulp as possible. Set aside.

Landfall

Season the scallops and turn them in 2 tsp vanilla oil. Warm four soup plates and arrange the uncooked scallops on them. Heat the cauliflower cream to boiling point. If too thick, add a little water. Liquidize using the blender. When piping hot, pour straight onto the scallops. Drizzle fine lines of vanilla oil on the surface. Sprinkle with Espelette pepper (Galley Pantry 2). Serve.

Cream

Galley Pantry 3
Vanilla Oil
½ cup (12 cl) grape-seed oil
2 vanilla beans (pods)

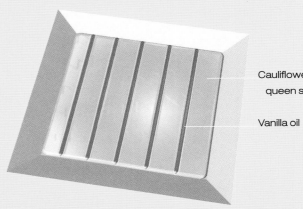

Cauliflower cream and queen scallops

Vanilla oil

Setting the Course—Every year when the lilac is in flower, a mass of cuttlefish invade the shallows of Cancale Bay. This little sea monster has a unique texture, somewhere between tender and firm. They are best cooked quickly over a wood fire, which gives them a very interesting smoked flavor. The citrus oil cuts in, and is then mollified by sweet vanilla; and a unique note is added by the zesty little Japanese lemon, the yuzu. But nothing could be more surprising than the licorice marshmallow of the cuttlefish itself.

Grilled Cuttlefish, Vanilla Oil, and Tar

Crew of 4

Rigging
Ribbed grill pan or barbecue
Fine-holed grater
Mason jar
Strainer
4 plates

Cruising Time
Prepare the vanilla oil the day before

From the Ship's Hold
Dry Jurançon

Provisions

Galley Pantry 1
4 small whole cuttlefish, 14 oz. (400 g) each,
    or 4 small squid

Galley Pantry 2
Vanilla Oil
½ cup (10 cl) grape-seed oil
½ vanilla bean (pod)
Zest of 2 yuzu lemons (available at Japanese groceries)
    or zest of 1 lemon + zest of 1 lime

May 2, 2004. Wind from the northwest, force 2 to 3. Smooth sea.

First Tack

Vanilla oil (Galley Pantry 2): Pour the grape-seed oil into the Mason jar, split open the vanilla bean and add it to the oil with the citrus zests. Close tightly and sterilize in a boiling-water bath for 10 minutes counting from the second boil. Leave jar in water to cool until next day.

Second Tack

Ideally, the cuttlefish should be bought fresh at the market, prepared towards the end of the morning, grilled on the embers of a lunchtime barbecue, and eaten in the cool of the same evening. Otherwise, prepare the cuttlefish a few hours before the meal (Galley Pantry 1). Cut open the body, remove the tentacles, heads, and guts. Set aside. Wash the mantle carefully under running water. Make incisions in the surface to stop it shrinking during cooking. Season and sear quickly on a hot grill to mark the flesh in both directions. Cut into ½ in. cubes.

Third Tack

Ink stock (Galley Pantry 3) and aromatic garnish: Recover the tentacles. Peel the garlic, then chop the spring onion and parsley finely. Cut the tentacles into largish chunks, wash and drain. Heat the olive oil in a pan, seal the tentacles briskly, then add the butter, garlic, onion, and parsley. Sauté for 2 minutes. Deglaze the pan with 2 tbs sherry vinegar and add the water and fish bouillon. Add the sterilized ink. Simmer gently for 30 minutes, then strain. Return to heat and reduce to 10 tbs black liquid.

Landfall

Warm the diced cuttlefish with the vanilla oil and the remaining 2 tbs sherry vinegar. Arrange the squares of cuttlefish on large warmed plates, and pour the vanilla oil on top. Drip pearls of the black stock into the oil. Place a few fleur de sel crystals on the cuttlefish squares and grate the yuzu zest over the plate. Serve.

gy Ink Stock

Galley Pantry 3
Ink Stock
Heads and trimmings of the 4 cuttlefish
1 tbs sterilized ink (available at groceries)
1 tbs olive oil
1 tbs (15 g) salted butter

Aromatic Garnish
1 clove garlic
1 spring onion
2 sprigs parsley
2 tbs + 2 tsp sherry vinegar
1 cup (25 cl) water
½ cup (10 cl) fish bouillon

Galley Pantry 4
Finishing
Fleur de sel
1 yuzu lemon

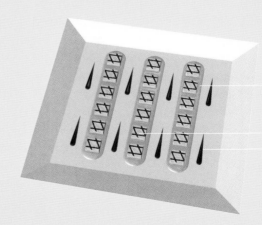

Vanilla oil

Cuttlefish square

Ink stock

Setting the Course—Here is the perfect recipe to rediscover the tastes of childhood. It will remind you of playing between the lines of redcurrants, stopping only to pop a little bunch of berries into your mouth, round and red like glass beads. Vanilla was the queen of flavors then; and later, at a more grownup age, came the discovery of bitter almond—and a rush of the same emotion. Not so very far from the Garden of Eden. . . .

Vanilla Cream with White Peaches

Crew of 4

Rigging
Sorbet maker
Strainer
Nonstick baking tray
Small handheld blender
4 small sake bowls
4 small glass yogurt pots
4 plates

Cruising Time
4 hours

From the Ship's Hold
Beaumes de Venise Muscat

Provisions

Galley Pantry 1
Vanilla Cream
1 cup (30 cl) milk
½ vanilla bean (pod)
3 tbs (45 g) sugar
3 egg yolks

Galley Pantry 2
Red Fruit Compote
2 oz. (60 g) blackcurrants
2 oz. (60 g) redcurrants
2 oz. (60 g) raspberries
1 tsp water
½ cup (120 g) sugar
½ tsp (8 g) agar-agar

July 9, 2004. Choppy seas. Wind from the northwest, force 3 to 4.

First Tack

Vanilla cream (Galley Pantry 1): Add the half vanilla bean to the milk and bring to the boil. Whisk together the egg yolks and sugar. Pour on the boiling milk, stirring constantly. Strain. Fill the yogurt pots to three-quarters full with this concoction and place them in a baking pan with an inch of water. Cook in a preheated oven at 300°F (150°C) until set. Cool to room temperature and refrigerate.

Second Tack

Red fruit compote (Galley Pantry 2): Gently stew the fruits with the water and sugar for about 15 minutes, then add the agar-agar. Set aside.

Third Tack

Almond tuile biscuits (Galley Pantry 3): Place the sugar, flour, egg whites, vanilla, and flaked almonds in a mixing bowl. Refrigerate for 2 hours. Melt the butter and add to the mixture while still warm. Preheat oven to 325°F (160°C). Spread thin circles of the mixture—the width of the yogurt pots—onto the baking sheet, until there is none left. Bake until golden brown. Remove with spatula. Keep in an airtight container.

Fourth Tack

Plum-kernel emulsion (Galley Pantry 4): Mix together the water, egg white, sugar, and lemon juice. Mix with the handheld blender, gradually pouring in the grape-seed and plum-kernel oil. Set aside.

Fifth Tack

Poached peaches (Galley Pantry 5): Plunge the peaches into boiling water for a few seconds. Run under cold water, peel and halve. Make a syrup with the water, sugar, and vanilla. Add the peaches and poach over a low heat for 5 minutes.

Landfall

Warm the plum-kernel emulsion in a small pan, whisking constantly. Add a few drops of water if too thick. Prepare large, square plates. Make a line of red fruit compote on one side. Place the two peach halves in the middle. Add a drop of plum-kernel dressing. Place the pot of vanilla cream on the right and top it with the rest of the red fruit compote. Cover with an almond tuile biscuit. Pour the rest of the warm plum-kernel dressing into a small sake bowl. Serve.

Galley Pantry 3
Almond Tuile Biscuits
7 tbs (100 g) sugar
½ cup (50 g) sifted plain flour
2 egg whites
¼ vanilla bean (pod)
⅔ cup (50 g) flaked almonds
4 tbs (50 g) melted butter

Galley Pantry 4
Plum-Kernel Emulsion
1 egg white
½ cup (10 cl) water
1 tbs sugar
3 tbs (5 cl) lemon juice
10 tbs (15 cl) grape-seed oil
½ cup (10 cl) plum-kernel oil (available at groceries)

Galley Pantry 5
Poached Peaches
4 white peaches
⅔ cup (150 g) sugar
1 ¼ cups (300 g) water
¼ vanilla bean (pod)

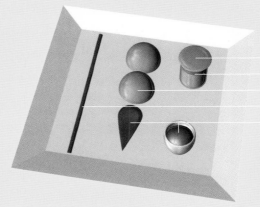

Almond tuile
Small pot of vanilla cream
Peach
Red fruit compote
Plum-kernel emulsion

Setting the Course—We have been making salted butter caramel for years in our kitchens. Its flavor is rendered even fuller, richer, and longer by the use of a vanilla of excellent quality. For this composition, I wanted to find a way of enjoying it as a "pick-me-up," at five o'clock on a winter's evening—like hot chocolate. But here it's to warm me up after a walk along the shore in late spring.

First Tack
Salted butter caramel (Galley Pantry 1): Place the sugar and glucose in a pan and caramelize together until light brown. Remove from heat and add the butter and cream (watch out for splashback). Add the quarter vanilla bean, split along its length. Stir over the heat until it reaches firm-ball stage, or 245–50°F (120°C) on a candy thermometer. Pour into the tray and leave to harden.

Second Tack
When cool, cut the caramel into ½-in. (1-cm) squares. Drop them into the milk (Galley Pantry 2). Bring to the boil, mixing with a whisk.

Landfall
Whisk this delightful milky treat until smooth.

Frothy Vanilla Milk with Salted Butter Caramel

Crew of 4

Rigging
Small handheld blender
Candy thermometer
Stainless-steel tray 4 x 2 in.
 (10 x 4 cm), 1 in. (2 cm) deep
4 hot-chocolate mugs

Cruising Time
4 hours

Provisions

Galley Pantry 1
Salted Butter Caramel
These caramels are available from
Les Maisons de Bricourt.
⅔ cup (150 g) sugar
⅔ cup (150 g) glucose
½ cup (100 g) salted butter
½ cup (100 g) cream
¼ bourbon vanilla bean (pod)

Galley Pantry 2
2 cups (½ liter) semi-skimmed milk

May 22, 2004. Fine, dry, cold weather. Stiff east wind, force 4 to 5.

Pineapples:
The original exotic fruit
latitude 19°23'60" N, longitude 99°2'60" W

Central America. Pineapples are native to Central America. It is said that Christopher Columbus first tasted pineapple when he landed in Guadeloupe in 1493.

204

208–209
Lobster Pieces, Pineapple, and
Salted Butter

210–211
Tropical Island Fruits, White
Pepper, and Orange-Flower Sorbet

History

Pineapples are native to Central America.

It is said that Christopher Columbus first tasted pineapple when he landed in Guadeloupe in 1493. However, the earliest proven discovery of pineapples by a European came in 1555, when a Huguenot explorer named Jean de Lery landed on the coast of Brazil. The French word for pineapple, *ananas*, is a deformation of the Tupi Indian term *nana*.

Pineapples were first brought back to Britain. They quickly became extremely fashionable in all the great European courts. Many museums preserve decorative objects in china and precious metals in the shape of a pineapple. They were also used as a pattern on tapestries and ladies' gowns.

It was not until after World War II that pineapples began to feature regularly on market stalls. To this day, they are still seen as exotic and something of a luxury.

Natural history

The pineapple is the fruit of a hardy perennial that belongs to the *Bromeliaceae* family. It is very distinctive with its orange-brown diamond-shaped segments and its crown of tough, spiky leaves. Some ten varieties are grown commercially.

Qualities

The Tupi Indians were quite right to name the fruit *nana*, which also means "sweet scent" in their language. Cut pineapple slices have a mouth-watering aroma that hints at the sweetness of the fruit.

Pineapples are naturally very sweet, but they are also very acidic. Cooked pineapple is less acidic and the flavor takes on the more complex taste of burnt sugar or molasses.

Uses

Whenever I am traveling in a tropical country, I like to stop off at one of the many roadside stalls for a slice of pineapple fresh from the fields. I always admire the dexterity of the farmers who peel and chop the flesh with a long, thin blade before presenting it with a broad smile.

I love using pineapple in my desserts. One of my favorite ways to use it is cold in a fruit soup. It marries extremely well with rum and with all manner of tropical fruits in salads. I also love oven-roast pineapple. Dotted with butter, basted with a sugar-syrup and with a dash of lemon and a pinch of nutmeg, it is a real treat.

Pineapple's firm texture, rich aroma, and acidic taste make it the perfect companion for a number of savory dishes. It is particularly good in chutneys. It also goes surprisingly well with lobster and crayfish. There are more ways to use pineapple than you might think!

The finest pineapples

Pineapples are exported either by airplane or by ship. Pineapples imported by airplane will have been harvested ripe and packaged and exported within twenty-four hours. They are riper and therefore have more taste than those exported by ship, which are harvested earlier. My favorite variety is the Victoria, the small, sweet pineapples with a rich aroma that grow on all small tropical islands. Unfortunately, this variety is rarely exported as the locals eat the harvest themselves. The three best-known varieties are as follows:

- Cayenne pineapples are excellent. These long, golden pineapples are grown in the Ivory Coast and in Martinique.

- The Queen variety is similar in shape to Cayenne pineapples, but is greener in color. The flesh is more acidic and less fruity in flavor. Queen pineapples are grown in the West Indies.

- The Red Spanish variety is purplish-red in color. The flesh is almost white and has less taste than the other two varieties.

Health benefits

Pineapple contains bromelain, which fights against muscle pain. Athletes often eat pineapple before competitions because of this. Pineapple is also good for digestion, since its proteolytic enzymes help break down the protein molecules in meat and the starch in potatoes, pasta, and the like. Pineapple can also be eaten as part of a weight-loss program.

Setting the Course—While flicking through some old magazines left in a locker on board, I came across an article about the pineapples they used to grow in greenhouses around Saint-Malo between the wars. An illustration showed the fronds of these tropical plants intertwined with the industrial elegance of those glass and steel constructions. Perhaps this dish echoes the nonchalance of the roaring Twenties, when this exotic fruit symbolized a certain luxury, just as lobster did—and still does. With its slightly acidic tang of English fruit-drops, I can well imagine a bit of snobbery must have entered into the eating of pineapple.

Lobster Pieces, Pineapple, and Salted

208

Crew of 4

Rigging
Broad, rigid knife for slicing
Wax paper
Strainer
4 soup plates

Cruising Time
2 hours

From the Ship's Hold
Condrieu or Alsace Pinot-Gris

Provisions

Galley Pantry 1
2 female lobsters weighing 2 lb. (1 kg) each
4 tbs (50 g) salted butter

Galley Pantry 2
1 pineapple

October 17, 2002. North wind, force 5 to 6. Rough sea.

First Tack
Scald the lobsters in boiling water for 1 minute. Separate the heads and claws from the bodies. Split the heads in two and remove the sand pouches. Crush the heads.

Second Tack
Sauce (Galley Pantry 3): Sauté the shells in the butter and sunflower oil until red. Make a caramel with the sugar. Add the shells. Deglaze the pan with the wine (watch out for splashing), and the chicken bouillon. Add the garlic, vanilla, lemon and orange juice and zest, and the 2 cumbava leaves. Leave for 20 minutes to simmer down to 8 tbs of liquid. Strain, pressing out as much sauce as possible.

Third Tack
Peel the pineapple (Galley Pantry 2) and cut into very fine strips, like tagliatelle. Keep any juice aside for the sauce.

Fourth Tack
Put the rice (Galley Pantry 4) in a pan and cover with double the volume of water (about ⅔ cup). Bring to boil and simmer gently, covered, for 20 minutes, making sure it doesn't stick. On a baking tray lined with wax paper, use a spatula to make 2 in. (1 cm) squares of rice, 1 grain thick. Dry in the oven at 200°F (100°C) for 1 hour. Heat the oil in a small pan and fry the dried rice squares one by one. Lift out with a slotted spoon and leave to drain on paper towel. The result should be little squares of puffed rice.

Landfall
Cut each lobster tail into 4. Sauté the tail pieces and claws in salted butter (Galley Pantry 1) for about 3 minutes on each side. Place in a baking pan and bake in a preheated oven at 200°F (100°C). Deglaze the pan with the sauce base and juice from the pineapple. Bring to boil and check seasoning. Serve in warmed soup plates, placing 1 claw and 2 tail pieces in each, with a few strips of pineapple and a puffed rice square. Cover the lobster with the tangy sauce. Serve.

Butter

Galley Pantry 3
Sauce
4 tbs (50 g) salted butter
¼ cup (5 cl) sunflower oil
1 tbs sugar
3 tbs (5 cl) dessert wine such as Coteaux du Layon
½ cup (10 cl) chicken bouillon
1 clove garlic, roasted
¼ vanilla bean (pod)
1 lemon
½ orange
2 cumbava leaves

Galley Pantry 4
⅓ cup (100 g) glutinous rice (available at Asian groceries)
1 cup (20 cl) sunflower oil

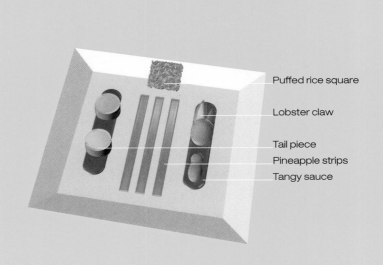

Puffed rice square

Lobster claw

Tail piece
Pineapple strips
Tangy sauce

Setting the Course—I look out of the window through the damp fog of this winter day and try to imagine myself elsewhere. I like to cuddle up by the granite fireplace, watch the glowing logs, and set off in search of distant sun. Pepper and orange-flower water have come a long way together over the centuries. Their journey took them across deserts; then they took to the sea, landing in Aswan or Lisbon. It is wonderful that fruits can still make us daydream by infusing our winter days with their scent. And I like to enjoy them in front of the fire, with the violence of the storm lashing against the windows.

Tropical Island Fruits, White Pepper

Crew of 4

Rigging
Airtight container
Nonstick baking sheet
Strainer
Small spatula
Sorbet maker
Stainless-steel cylinder, 8 in. (20 cm) long,
    ½ in. (1.5 cm) thick
Pastry cutter, 8 in. (20 cm) x 2 in. (5.5 cm)
4 shallow, wide-rimmed champagne glasses

Cruising Time
8 hours

From the Ship's Hold
Sweet Gaillac

Provisions

Galley Pantry 1
Hibiscus Jelly
½ cup (10 cl) water
2 tbs sugar
2 tbs dried hibiscus flowers
3 tsp agar-agar, or seaweed gelatin

Galley Pantry 2
Strong Passion-Fruit Juice
3 tbs (4 cl) water
4 tsp sugar
7 tbs passion-fruit pulp

December 22, 2003. Wind from the southwest, force 4 to 5. Visibility practically nil. Continuous drizzle.

First Tack

Hibiscus jelly (Galley Pantry 1): Make a syrup with the sugar and water. Bring to boil, remove from heat, and add the hibiscus flowers. Leave to infuse for 10 minutes, then strain. When the syrup is lukewarm, add the agar-agar. Pour into champagne glasses and refrigerate.

Second Tack

Strong passion-fruit juice (Galley Pantry 2): Bring the sugar and water to the boil, remove from heat and mix in the passion-fruit pulp. Bring back to the boil and simmer for 5 minutes on a low heat. Cool.

Third Tack

Yogurt sorbet (Galley Pantry 3): Bring the water, glucose, and sugar mixture to the boil. Cool. Add the yogurt and lemon juice, then the white pepper and orange-flower water. Pour into the sorbet maker. When made, set aside in freezer.

Fourth Tack

Fresh exotic fruits (Galley Pantry 4): Cut the pineapple, mango, banana, and kiwis into cubes. Spoon out the passion-fruit flesh. Mix the fruit in a bowl and refrigerate.

Fifth Tack

Crunchy passion-fruit tuiles (Galley Pantry 5): Flatten out the softened butter, sift the confectioner's sugar onto it, add the passion-fruit juice, and finally incorporate the flour. Mix together thoroughly. Use the rectangular pastry cutter to get regularly shaped tuiles. Place it on the nonstick baking sheet and spread a thin layer of dough into the bottom with the spatula. Repeat the operation 4 times. Preheat oven to 325°F (165°C). Bake until golden. Allow the tuiles to cool on the tray for a minute, then roll each one around the cylinder. Cool. Store in the airtight container.

Landfall

Arrange the tropical fruit in the champagne glasses. Add a scoop of white pepper yogurt sorbet. Sprinkle on a fine line of pepper. Place a crunchy passion-fruit tuile on the edge of each glass. Serve.

and Orange-Flower Sorbet

Galley Pantry 3
Yogurt Sorbet
¾ cup (17 cl) water
2 tsp glucose
½ cup (100 g) sugar
1 pot plain yogurt (125 g)
4 tsp lemon juice
5 turns freshly-ground white pepper
1 tsp orange-flower water

Galley Pantry 4
Fresh Exotic Fruits
½ pineapple
¼ mango
½ banana
2 kiwis
2 passion fruits

Galley Pantry 5
Crunchy Passion-Fruit Tuiles
3 tbs (40 g) softened butter
¾ cup (100 g) confectioner's sugar
1 ½ oz. (50 g) fresh passion-fruit juice
3 tbs flour

Crunchy passion-fruit tuile

Yogurt sorbet

Fruits

Hibiscus jelly

Oranges: Bitter-sweet
latitude 22°11'60" N, longitude 113°32'60" E

China and India. Oranges are native to the thick forests that cover the high plateaus of China and India. The bitter oranges known as Seville oranges (the fruit of the bitter orange tree) were brought to the Mediterranean basin by Arab traders.

History

Oranges are native to the thick forests that cover the high plateaus of China and India. The bitter oranges known as Seville oranges (the fruit of the bitter orange tree) were brought to the Mediterranean basin by Arab traders. Monks are known to have grown these trees in their walled monastery gardens in the early Middle Ages.

Sweet oranges are originally from China. They arrived in Europe much later. The first Crusaders discovered the sweet fruit in Palestine. Later, Vasco da Gama brought oranges to Spain where the new fruit soon became very popular. Orange trees were planted in great quantities during the Renaissance and quickly adapted to the local climate. It is curious to note that, at the same time, orange trees were grown in orangeries elsewhere in Europe, but only as decorative plants. Louis XIV of France is said to have loved their perfume so much that he ordered an orange tree to be placed in each corridor at

 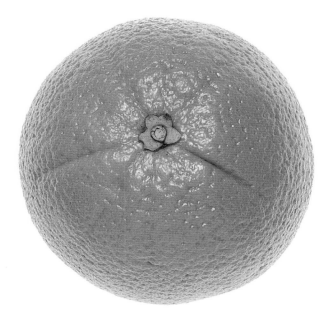

Versailles. It was not until the nineteenth century that oranges became widely known in northern Europe in the form of desserts and breakfast marmalade.

Today, Europe produces vast quantities of oranges. Spain is one of the world's leading producers. While they are now considered rather ordinary, not so long ago an orange in a Christmas stocking was considered a real treat.

Natural history

Bitter Seville oranges and sweet oranges are the fruit of a tree of the *Aurantiaceae* family. The orange, lumpy peel protects a heart of juicy pulp divided into segments.

Qualities

The juice is what gives the orange its taste, which can vary from extremely acid to delightfully sweet. Orange-flower water is extracted from the blossom of the bitter orange tree. Its heady perfume is a perfect match for milk-based desserts.

Uses

Bitter Seville oranges are used in jams and sweets, although these days an artificial flavoring is often used instead. They are also used in jellies and can be used instead of lemons in sauces and vinaigrettes. It is a shame that Seville oranges are not more widely used in the kitchen. People often forget that they were the original sweet-and-sour ingredient.

I like marrying oranges and shellfish, and I add the zest of an orange to all my bouillons and seafood sauces.

The finest oranges

Navel oranges are the best sweet oranges. They take their name from the second rudimentary berry found within the orange where the blossom was attached: the "navel." The best blood oranges are three varieties grown in Sicily—moro, taroco, and sanguinelle. For bitter oranges, I recommend the fruit of the citron tree that grows in Lebanon.

Health benefits

Oranges are particularly rich in vitamins A, B, and C as well as potassium, calcium, and phosphorus.

Setting the Course—Who has never been tempted, on coming to the end of a pile of moules marinières, to grab the nearest spoon and drink up the juice at the bottom of the dish? The temptation with clams is even stronger, for the juice is more subtle. Its delicacy will engulf you like the taste of the waves themselves: sharp, peppery, and lemony because of the ginger. I like to serve it with these small, delicate fillets of sole, coupled with the welcome smoothness of a light orange sauce.

First Tack

Two hours before the meal, prepare the marinière (Galley Pantry 2). Rinse the cockles in clear water for 30 minutes. Preheat a high-sided pan, throw in the cockles and the 8 tbs dessert wine, cover and cook on a high heat for 5 minutes. Recover and strain the juice. The cockles can be discarded. For the aromatic garnish: peel and slice the shallot, garlic, and ginger. Chop the onion and the parsley.

Soften the rest of the garnish in the butter for 5 minutes, and add the remaining 3 tbs wine. Rapidly reduce to half, then add the juice from the cockles and the fish bouillon. Reduce again by one-third. Strain, cool and refrigerate.

Second Tack

Scrub the new potatoes (Galley Pantry 4) and boil them in their skins. Peel while still hot, and cool in iced water.

Sole Marinière with Clams and Orang

Crew of 4

Rigging
Small handheld blender
Strainer
Fine-holed grater
Nonstick frying pan
4 soup plates

Cruising Time
4 hours

From the Ship's Hold
White Saint Joseph

Provisions

Galley Pantry 1
8 small whole soles
16 clams

Galley Pantry 2
Marinière
7 oz. (200 g) cockles
8 tbs + 3 tbs dessert wine, such as Coteaux du Layon
1 large knob of butter
1 shallot
½ clove garlic
1 knob fresh ginger
1 spring onion
2 sprigs parsley
5 tbs fish bouillon

April 22, 2003. Force 4 to 5 west wind. Sea moderate to rough.

Drain and set aside in a pan. Trim and wash the Chinese cabbage. Chop the chives and parsley very finely, and shred the chervil. Set aside. Start to heat the vegetable bouillon in a saucepan, ready for reheating the potatoes and cooking the Chinese leaf.

Third Tack

Orange dressing (Galley Pantry 3): Poach the egg for 2 minutes in just-boiling water with a little vinegar added. Leave to cool. Grate the zest of one of the oranges. Squeeze both oranges and strain the juice. Place the poached egg, orange juice, and zest in a high-sided bowl and blend with the handheld blender, adding the grape-seed oil a little at a time. Season the resulting emulsion and set aside.

Fourth Tack

Prepare the soles (Galley Pantry 1). Remove the skin from both sides and fillet. The bones may be used for making fish bouillon. Open the clams. Remove half of them completely from their shells, and leave the rest attached to one shell. Recover as much juice as possible and strain it into a pan. Add the clams, ready to reheat.

Landfall

Bring the vegetable bouillon to boil, add to the potatoes and reheat to boiling point. Preheat the frying pan, remove from heat and cook the seasoned sole fillets very gently on both sides for about 3 minutes. Reheat the marinière. Heat up the orange dressing, which will thicken as it warms. Five minutes before serving, warm the clams in their juices, without boiling. Put the Chinese cabbage in with the potatoes. Warm 4 large soup plates. Lay out the sole fillets on two-thirds of the plate. Add the herbs to the marinière. Drain the potatoes and Chinese cabbage and alternate on the remaining third of the plate. Arrange the clams. Add a little clam juice to the marinière and pour generously into the plates. Transfer the orange dressing into a sauceboat and serve separately. Diners will pour a spoonful of orange emulsion onto the corner of their plate, which will gradually run into the marinière.

Dressing

Galley Pantry 3
Orange Dressing
1 egg
2 oranges
6 tbs grape-seed oil

Galley Pantry 4
Garnish
12 small new potatoes
12 leaves Chinese cabbage
1 tbs finely chopped chives
1 tbs chervil sprigs
1 tbs chopped flat parsley
2 cups (½ liter) vegetable bouillon

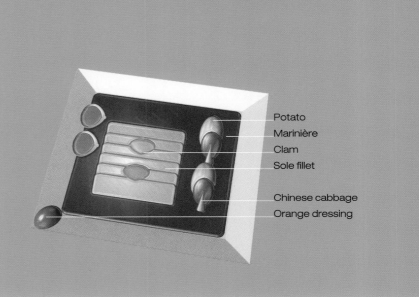

Potato
Marinière
Clam
Sole fillet

Chinese cabbage
Orange dressing

Setting the Course—Emmanuel, one of my assistants who is passionate about vegetables, brought the basis of this surprising dish to me one day, and we have since refined it together. His initial idea was to bring together vegetables and seaweed and rely on the "intelligent bitterness" of orange. To begin with, we took our cue from Mauritius and the sweet-savory-hot mixture that is achar, or vegetable pickle. Our adventure brought us back, little by little, to our own shores and our vegetable garden.

First Tack
Four days before the meal, prepare the seeds for sprouting. Soak the fenugreek seeds (Galley Pantry 4) overnight. The following day, place them in the seed-sprouting tray to germinate.

Second Tack
The vegetable mix is prepared 48 hours before the meal (Galley Pantry 1). Peel and grate the carrots. Wash the zucchini, cut into four lengthwise, remove the seeds, and grate. Peel the cucumber and prepare in the same way. Cut the half-bulb of fennel in half again and grate it from the outside, holding by the middle part. The other vegetables have to be chopped by hand. Wash the celery and slice finely. Wash, halve, and slice the mushrooms. Cut the pepper into four, remove the seeds and white pith, peel and bell dice. Set the pepper aside. Put all the other vegetables except the green beans into a bowl and sprinkle with salt (Galley Pantry 2). Refrigerate for 30 minutes.

Briny Orange

Crew of 4

Rigging
Small handheld blender
Large-holed grater
Vegetable peeler
Scissors
Seed-sprouting tray
4 plates

Cruising Time
4 days

From the Ship's Hold
Alsace Pinot Gris

Provisions

Galley Pantry 1
Vegetable Mix
2 carrots
1 zucchini
½ cucumber
½ bulb fennel
2 sticks celery
5 large white field mushrooms
1 red bell pepper
1 handful fresh fine green beans

July 5, 2004. Light northerly breeze, force 2 to 3. Clear skies and smooth sea.

Third Tack

While the mixture is being salted, prepare the achar marinade (Galley Pantry 2). Peel the 4 oranges with the vegetable peeler, taking as little white skin as possible. Place the peel in a high-sided bowl. Squeeze the oranges and put half the juice in the bowl with the peel, keeping half aside for the onion and nori compote. Peel the garlic and add it to the bowl. Add the grape-seed oil, thyme, turmeric, chilli, and salt. Mix with the handheld blender until the zest is very finely chopped. Transfer this mixture to a pan large enough to hold all the mixed vegetables. Set aside.

The onion and nori compote is prepared 48 hours before the meal (Galley Pantry 3). Halve the onions and chop very finely. Cut the nori into very fine strips with the scissors. Sweat the onions with the olive oil, and add the nori, keeping some back for finishing the plates. Add the juice of 2 oranges, the soy sauce, water, and muscovado sugar. Cook very gently until all the juice has been absorbed. Cool and refrigerate.

Fourth Tack

Finish the vegetable mix. Rinse the vegetables thoroughly under running water and soak in plenty of fresh water for 15 minutes, then drain well. Cooking the marinade: Heat the oil in a pan; when it begins to crackle, add the diced bell pepper. Cook for one minute, then add the remaining orange juice. Mix in the vegetables, add the currants (Galley Pantry 4), and mix again. Cook for no more than 3 minutes and then remove from heat. Add the rice vinegar (Galley Pantry 2). Refrigerate until the meal is ready to serve.

Landfall

Present on cold plates. Just before serving, cut the green beans in half lengthwise, then in half again widthwise, then cut into 1-in. (2-cm) pieces (a tedious process, but necessary). Add the raw green beans to the vegetable mix with one-third of the fenugreek sprouts. Mix well. Lay out 5 narrow lines of vegetable mix. Alternate with fine lines of onion and nori compote, adding flakes of nori on top of these lines. Add a few clusters of fenugreek sprouts. Serve.

Galley Pantry 2
Achar Marinade
4 oranges
1 clove garlic
1 cup (25 cl) grape-seed oil
1 tsp dried thyme
Dash of turmeric
Dash of hot chilli
2 tsp salt
2 tbs rice vinegar

Galley Pantry 3
Onion and Seaweed Compote
6 spring onions
3 sheets nori (sushi seaweed)
2 tbs olive oil
Juice of 2 oranges (from Galley Pantry 2)
2 tbs soy sauce
2 tbs water
1 tbs muscovado sugar

Galley Pantry 4
2 tbs fenugreek sprouts
3 tbs currants

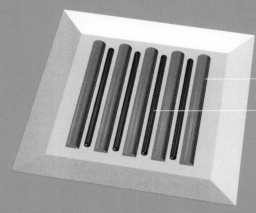

Vegetable mix

Onion and seaweed compote

Setting the Course—While traveling in India with my friends Michel and Ginette Bras, I was fascinated to observe the rather magical expertise that the Indians have acquired over the centuries in terms of the transformation of milk through various stages, particularly yogurt. In the little stalls in Jaipur and Calcutta, I saw milk being worked in curious and interesting ways. I often think of that when working on some of my desserts. In this recipe, I tease the Indians somewhat by associating a flavored milk with the very special "atmosphere" of orange marmalade, a quintessential product of the colonial British Raj. As a final touch in this dessert, I include milk in another of its forms: a fragrant scoop of ice cream. And the presence of almond evokes Muslim culture, so very present in India.

Oranges, Fresh Almonds, and Rose

224

Crew of 4

Rigging
Sorbet maker
Small handheld blender
Ladle
Strainer
Cooking thermometer
4 small bowls
4 small plates

Cruising Time
24 hours

From the Ship's Hold
Sainte Croix du Mont

Provisions

Galley Pantry 1
Orange Marmalade
3 oranges
1 cup (230 g) sugar
¾ cup (17 cl) water

Galley Pantry 2
Rosemary Milk
1 ½ cups (40 cl) whole milk
1 small sprig fresh rosemary
3 drops rennet

July 2, 2003. Light easterly breeze, force 2 to 3. Early mist lifting. Fine, good visibility.

First Tack

Orange marmalade (Galley Pantry 1): Wash the oranges. Quarter and chop as finely as possible. Add the sugar, and leave to candy overnight at room temperature. The following day, add the water and cook the marmalade for 1 hour in a saucepan. Set aside.

Second Tack

Rosemary milk (Galley Pantry 2): Heat the milk to 95°F (35°C). Stir in the rennet. Add the sprig of rosemary and allow to infuse for 5 minutes. Strain into the small bowls, filling three-quarters full. Maintain at 95°F (35°C) for 45 minutes, as when making yogurt. Set aside.

Third Tack

Bitter-almond ice cream (Galley Pantry 3): Heat the milk and cream. Add the sugar and powdered milk. Bring to boil and remove from heat. When temperature falls to around 120°F (50°C), whisk in the butter. Blend in the marzipan and pulverized almonds. Add a few drops of bitter almond extract. Pour into sorbet maker.

Landfall

Add a layer of orange marmalade to the bowls. Top with bitter-almond ice cream and a teaspoon of fresh chopped almonds. Serve.

mary Milk

Galley Pantry 3
Bitter-almond Ice Cream

1 ½ cups (35 cl) milk
3 tbs cream
5 tbs caster sugar
2 tbs powdered milk
1 ½ tbs (20 g) butter
1 tbs (15 g) marzipan (70% almonds)
9 tbs pulverized almonds
A few drops of bitter-almond extract
2 tbs fresh chopped almonds

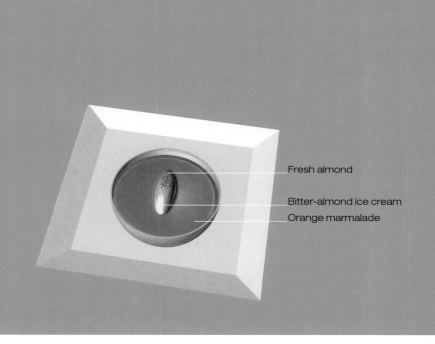

Fresh almond

Bitter-almond ice cream

Orange marmalade

Strawberries: Sweet berries
latitude 33°2'52" S, longitude 71°36'4" W

North and South America, Asia, Europe. Wild strawberries are found throughout the Americas, Asia, and Europe, from Cape Horn to the Shetland Islands.

History

Wild strawberries are found throughout the Americas, Asia, and Europe, from Cape Horn to the Shetland Islands. They were spread by birds, which are extremely fond of the juicy red berries.

Wild strawberries were much appreciated in Greek and Roman times, but it was not until the late Middle Ages that strawberry plants began to be cultivated in gardens. In 1588, Thomas Hariot, an English explorer in America, noted in his diary that he had discovered strawberries "as good and great as those which we have in English gardens," which suggests the fruit were then being cultivated. By the early 1800s, Americans were cultivating strawberries at home in their gardens, but because the fruit were too delicate for transport, the produce was only sold locally. The first long-distance shipping of strawberries across the U.S. occurred in 1843 when some innovative farmers from Cincinatti spread ice on top of the strawberry boxes and sold them across the country. Nowadays, strawberries are available all year-round. Thanks to careful selection, strawberries are now bigger and redder than ever. Unfortunately, a number of the modern varieties are completely lacking in taste.

Natural history

Altogether, there are more than six hundred varieties of strawberries. In fact, in botanical terms, strawberries are neither a true fruit nor a vegetable, but a type of hardy grass from the *Fragaria* family. The true fruits of the strawberry plant are in fact the small, hard, yellow pips on the outside of the strawberry.

Qualities

Strawberries have a sweet, subtle, delicate taste. The texture is very important: they should be tender but firm. Good strawberries are never floury or grainy.

Uses

Strawberries are at their best served as nature intended. I take them out of the refrigerator two hours before serving so they warm to room temperature, scattering with a little sugar and perhaps adding a piece of star anise and a squeeze of lemon. I serve them cut in half with a dribble of honey, a twist of freshly-ground white pepper, and a splash of cider vinegar added at the very last moment. The most important thing to make sure of is the quality of the berries, which should be as fresh as possible.

The finest strawberries

The variety known as Mara des Bois, bred in the 1990s, is a large strawberry that tastes like wild fruit. It is excellent if not forced too early. The early Surprise des Halles variety has a deliciously tart bite. Vicomtesse Héricart de Thury strawberries are subtle, juicy, sweet, and intense. The latter variety is sadly becoming increasingly rare, as the yields are very low.

Health benefits

Strawberries are rich in vitamin C and iron. They are refreshing and have a depurative effect, and are recommended in cases of diabetes and kidney and hepatic disorders. People with known food allergies should take care, as strawberries have been known to trigger rashes and other allergic reactions.

Setting the Course—When the first glimmers of spring return, I savor the moment as a new lease on life. Good strawberries and rhubarb arrive in the markets at the same time. I created this fresh and invigorating composition to help us to "wash away" the bleakness of winter. I see it as a wave, urged on by the sharp flavor of the cumbava, this little citrus fruit from Thailand that I adore.

Strawberries, Rhubarb Water, Rhubarb

Crew of 4

Rigging
Small handheld blender
Sorbet maker
4 stainless-steel pastry molds, 2 in. (5 cm) high,
   1 ½ in. (4.5 cm) across
Round pastry-cutter, 1 ¼ in. (3 cm) across
Nonstick baking tray
Purée-strainer
Airtight container
4 bowls

Cruising Time
24 hours

From the Ship's Hold
Côteaux du Layon

Provisions

Galley Pantry 1
Strawberry Mousse
1 lb. (500 g) strawberries (Mara des Bois, if possible)
4 tbs sugar
1 tsp (14 g) agar-agar (seaweed gelatin)

Galley Pantry 2
2 lb. (1 kg) rhubarb
1 cup (200 g) sugar

Galley Pantry 3
Rhubarb-and-Cumbava Sorbet
1 cup (250 g) water
1 ½ cups (260 g) sugar
10 cumbava leaves

May 2, 2003. Gentle breeze from the north, force 2 to 3. Fine weather, sea calm.

First Tack

Strawberry mousse (Galley Pantry 1): Mix the strawberries and sugar together in a bowl. Leave overnight to macerate. Liquidize with the handheld blender. Warm the pulp and add the agar-agar. Filter through the purée strainer, pressing juice from the pulp. Half-fill the 4 pastry molds. Refrigerate.

Second Tack

Preparing the rhubarb (Galley Pantry 2): Peel the rhubarb. Cut into chunks and mix with the sugar. Leave for 24 hours to macerate. Cook over a low heat and allow to cool. Drain, reserving the juice for the rhubarb water (Fourth Tack). Reserve 1 lb. (500 g) cooked rhubarb for the sorbet. The rest is used in the "Landfall."

Third Tack

Rhubarb and cumbava sorbet (Galley Pantry 3): Purée the remaining rhubarb with the handheld blender. Make a syrup with the water, sugar, and chopped cumbava leaves. Bring to the boil, then cool and strain through purée strainer. Mix 1 ⅓ cups (300 g) of this syrup with the puréed rhubarb. Pour into the sorbet maker. When made, keep in freezer.

Fourth Tack

Rhubarb water (Galley Pantry 4): Make a syrup with the water, sugar, vanilla, and cumbava leaves. Bring to the boil and strain through purée-strainer. When the syrup has cooled, take 1 cup (250 g) of it and mix with 1 cup (250 g) rhubarb juice (Second Tack). Refrigerate.

Fifth Tack

Dried mango (Galley Pantry 5): Peel, stone and liquidize the mango. Using the pastry-cutter to ensure neat edges, spread a very thin layer of mango purée on the baking sheet to make 16 mango pastilles. Dry in the oven at 200°F (90°C) for 2 hours. The resulting mango pastilles should be translucent. When dry, remove one by one and keep in a dry place or airtight container.

Sixth Tack

Garnish (Galley Pantry 6): Peel the mango and cut into 24 slivers. Also cut the large strawberries into 24 segments.

Landfall

Set the strawberry mousse in the middle of the bowls. Surround with 6 small spoonfuls cooked rhubarb and the pieces of strawberry and mango. Pour on the rhubarb water. Carefully remove the pastry rings and place a spoonful of sorbet on top. Finish off with a few dried mango pastilles. Serve.

nd-Cumbava Sorbet

Galley Pantry 4
Rhubarb Water
½ cup (130 g) water
7 tbs (100 g) sugar
¼ vanilla bean (pod)
8 cumbava leaves

Galley Pantry 5
Dried Mango
1 very ripe mango

Galley Pantry 6
Garnish
1 mango
4 large strawberries

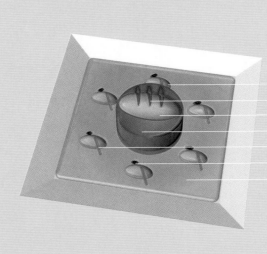

Rhubarb
Dried mango pastille
Sorbet
Strawberry mousse
Mango
Strawberry
Rhubarb water

Setting the Course—For me, the white peach is probably the best fruit in the world. Here, this elegant, delicately flavored beauty finds the small red fruits of the July garden at its feet. Chinon was Rabelais' favorite wine; just as the Romans did in ancient times, I like to flavor it with spices from the Orient and dream of the journeys of Alexander the Great. To be enjoyed on a summer evening when the cool of the night brings its first chill.

Red Berries from the Garden, Mulled

Crew of 4

Rigging
Strainer
Sorbet maker
Ladle
Small handheld blender
4 soup plates

Cruising Time
4 hours

Provisions

Galley Pantry 1
Mulled Wine
4 cups (1 liter) Chinon red wine
½ cinnamon stick
4 cardamom pods
4 star anise
2 cloves
1 ½ cups (300g) sugar
Zest of 2 oranges
Zest of 2 lemons

July 2, 2004. Light northeasterly breeze, force 2 to 3. Sea calm.

First tack

Mulled wine (Galley Pantry 1): Gently simmer together the red wine, spices, zests, and sugar for 30 minutes. Remove from the heat and leave to steep for 30 minutes. Strain and set aside.

Second tack

White peach sorbet (Galley Pantry 2): Plunge the peaches into boiling water for 2 minutes, then soak in iced water. This stops the cooking and allows the skin to be removed more easily. Remove the pits and chop the flesh with the handheld blender. Bring the water, sugar, glucose, and lemon juice to the boil. Mix this syrup with the peach flesh and pour into the sorbet maker.

Third tack

Fresh red berries from the garden (Galley Pantry 3): Wash the fruits and remove the stalks. Two hours before the meal, add them to the wine infusion.

Landfall

Warm the fruits in the wine and ladle them into large soup plates. Add a large scoop of peach sorbet. Serve.

Wine, and Peach Sorbet

Galley Pantry 2
White Peach Sorbet
1 lb. (500 g) white peaches
7 tbs (10 cl) water
½ cup (120 g) sugar
3 tbs (50 g) glucose
1 ½ tbs (24 g) lemon juice

Galley Pantry 3
Red Berries from the Garden
7 oz. (200g) strawberries
7 oz. (200g) redcurrants
7 oz. (200g) blackcurrants
7 oz. (200g) raspberries

Fruits in mulled wine

Peach sorbet

Spices from Rœllinger

My spices are created in an old eighteenth-century warehouse where I have been cooking for over twenty years. The spices, which come from the finest sources, are first dried and sterilized before being roasted, crushed, and ground up. Finally they are weighed, measured out, and blended into the spice powders that have made a name for our adventurous brand of cuisine which plunders the vegetable garden and the sea. To make it easier for everyone to make use of the full range of spices available to us all, I will

Blended Spices

Poudre Retour des Indes
Sprinkle over fish or crustaceans or use to flavor a sauce

Poudre Névis
Mix with an equal amount of breadcrumbs for breading fillets of fish and scallops

Poudre Grande Caravane
Use to flavor vegetables or lamb

Poudre de Neptune
Sprinkle over fish and mollusks or use to flavor a sauce

Poudre Rêve de Cochin
Add to fromage blanc or yogurt, use for marinating fish or seasoning vegetables for a salad

Poudre Curry Corsaire
Use to flavor cream sauces and to season mussels

Poudre Serinissima
Use to season tomates and ratatouille

Poudre d'Or
Use to season oysters and mollusks

Poudre des Fées
Use to flavor soups and broths

Poudre Gallo
Use to season poultry and white meats

Poudre du Voyage
Use to flavor beans, cauliflower, lentils, or creamed vegetables

Poudre Marine
Use to season fishes high in iodine, like mullet or mackerel

Poudre du Vent
Use to season squab or to flavor pastas with cream sauce

Poudre des Alizés
Use to flavor vinaigrettes

Oils

Huile et Cumbavas
Use just a few drops to flavor all types of seafood. Ingredients: grape-seed oil and cumbava

Huile Muscadée
Use to season pasta, fish, and scallops. Ingredients: grap-eseed oil, almond, nutmeg, and mace

Huile et Poivrons 'Niora'
Use to season tomatoes, pasta, fish, and shellfish. Ingredients: grape-seed oil and niora pepper

Huile et Fleurs de Sureau
Use to season fish

Huile et Agrumes
Use to give a citrus flavor to all types of seafood

Huile des Sirènes
Anise and seaweed flavoring for fish, shellfish, and vegetables

Vinaigre Celtique
Use just a few drops to add to the flavor of fish, pasta, potatoes, or cheeses

These products can be ordered from Maisons de Bricourt, 1 rue Duguesclin, 35260 Cancale. Tel: 00 33 (0)2 99 89 64 76. Fax: 00 33 (0)2 99 89 88 47. www.maisons-de-bricourt.com

continue to create new powders, ones which will call upon the resources of both earth and sea or convey the spirit of a season and perhaps even the unique tastes of a specific person. Just as a creator of perfume must develop his sense of smell, I have developed my sense of taste in a world of flavors. In my cooking, this has allowed me to express the adventurous spirit of my region and to travel not only as far as the eye can see but beyond the horizon, responding to the call of the sea.

Chutneys
Chutney de Tomates
This tomato chutney is a playful accompaniment to fish and vegetables

Chutney de Saint-Malo
For crustaceans, poultry, and cheeses

Poivre des Mondes
A balance of different peppers that brings together the singularity of each

Jardin Marin
A blend of seaweeds for vinaigrettes, bouillons, and sauces

Spice Infusions
Grog des Iles
Add cider, rum, and orange zest to create a maritime grog

Songe de Nuit
Herbal tea for children and adults

O.R.
Aromatherapy infusion with numerous benefits

Fish Stock
Provisions
2 leeks (white portion only), 1 carrot, 1 onion, 1 small rib celery 1 clove garlic, thyme, parsley, bay leaf, the peel from 1 orange, 1 knob fresh ginger, ⅔ cup well-flavored white wine, 1⅓ cups (400 g) fish bones (sole, preferably), 4 cups (1 liter) water.

Setting the Course
Rinse the fish bones in cold running water. Finely chop the carrot, onion, and white portion of the leeks. Cook gently in the butter until soft. Cover with the wine, bring to a boil, and simmer for 1 minute. Add the fish bones, cover with 4 cups water. Add the herbs, orange peel, and ginger. Slowly bring to the boil, reduce heat, and simmer for about 30 minutes without skimming so that clarification will take place naturally. At the end of the cooking period, strain carefully and refrigerate.

Landfall
This fish stock will keep, refrigerated, for 4 to 5 days. It can also be frozen in ice-cube trays. The cubes of stock may then be more easily used as needed.

Chicken Stock
Provisions
1 chicken
8 cups (2 liters) water
1 carrot
1 onion
1 shallot
1 leek
1 small rib celery
1 crushed clove garlic
A few sprigs parsley
½ in. (1 cm) cinnamon stick
10 black peppercorns
½ in. (1 cm) vanilla bean (pod)

Setting the Course
Finely chop the carrot, onion, leek, shallot, and celery rib. Place the chicken in a pot with the 8 cups of cold water, chopped vegetables, crushed garlic, cinnamon, peppercorns, and vanilla. Gradually bring to the boil, reduce heat, and simmer for 3 hours without skimming so that clarification will take place naturally. Strain.

Landfall
This chicken stock will keep, refrigerated, for 4 days. It can also be frozen in ice-cube trays. The cubes of stock may then be used as needed in any recipe calling for chicken stock.

Index of Recipes

Translated from the French by Louise Guiney, Susan Pickford,
and Joseph West
Copyediting: Penelope Isaac
Typesetting: Corinne App
Proofreading: Slade Smith
Illustrations: Georges Baur based on drawings by Emmánuel Tessier
and photographs by Alain Willaume
Color separation: Pacific & Co.

Distributed in North America by Rizzoli International Publications, Inc.

Simultaneously published in French as *Une Cuisine Contemporaine*
© Éditions Flammarion, 2005
English-language edition
© Éditions Flammarion, 2005

www.editions.flammarion.com

05 06 07 5 4 3 2

FC0488-05-XI
ISBN-13: 9782080304889
ISBN-10: 2-0803-0488-7
Dépôt légal: 08/2005

Printed in Italy by Canale

Acknowledgments

My warmest thanks go to Emmanuel Tessier,
second-in-command at Les Maisons de
Bricourt, for his unstinting work both on
the recipes and the 3-D images. Thanks must
also go to the whole team at Les Maisons
de Bricourt—the head pastry chef Jocelyne
Fallait, the head chef André Eslan, his deputy
Jérôme Aumont, Nicolas Penven, Damien
Loinsard, Jean-Daniel Morel, and Olivier
Deluc—who all worked hard on the project.
Many thanks to Fabienne Tizon, who pro-
duced a neat, and above all legible, printout
of my handwritten notes.

Grateful thanks also to all my suppliers
who provide me with the finest and freshest
vegetables and shellfish and the best of the
catch of the day; not forgetting all the
workers the world over who harvest and
process—often in difficult and dangerous
conditions—the pepper, ginger, cloves,
and other spices we take for granted.

Thanks also to Christian Chouamier of
Brittany Ferries, to Bruno Lassus, Commander
of the Port of Saint-Malo, and to Jean-Luc
Tachet, captain of the trawler Cap Pilar.
I must also thank Valhrona for the loan of
the cacao pods and beans and Duperier for
the foie gras.

Thanks to Henri Coudoux, at the Maison
européenne de la Photographie (Paris).
Thanks to Paul Cottin. Thanks to
Sodexho Alliance.

Finally, my deepest thanks to the photographers—and friends—Emmanuel Pierrot
and Michel Labelle, and to all of Georges
Catherine Dauriac's team and to the artists,
agencies and galleries who so kindly lent
their photographs of the sea to me.

Endpaper 2 4 6 10 12 42

64 88 102 114 136 138

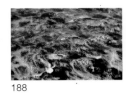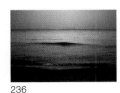

160 188 214 236 236 240 Endpaper

Endpapers: Alain Willaume, *De finibus terrae* series, 1991–2000. *Page 2:* Dolores Marat. *Page 4:* Alain Willaume, *Praia Grande,* 1984. *Pages 6 and 10:* Sonja Braas, *Forces #13,* 2002 and *Forces #1,* 2002. *Page 12:* Jorge Ribalta, *Untitled,* 1987. *Page 42:* Mayte Vieta, *Diptyque,* Museo de la Universidad de Alicante, MUA. *Page 64:* Joseph Kudelka/Magnum. *Page 88:* Harry Gruyaert, *La baie des anges,* 1988/Magnum. *Page 102:* Jean Gaumy, *La Manche - le remorqueur Abeille Languedoc,* 2000/Magnum. *Page 114:* Michel Labelle. *Page 136:* Werner Hannappel, courtesy of Michelle Chomette. *Page 138:* Michael Kenna, *Wave, Scarborough,* 1981, courtesy of Michelle Chomette. *Page 160:* Jean-Marc Tinguaud, *Naples,* 1986. *Page 188:* Philip Plisson. *Page 214:* Marie Bovo, *Plage, DD,* courtesy of Roger Pailhas Gallery. *Page 236:* Bernard Plossu, courtesy of Michelle Chomette. *Page 240:* Juan Manuel Castro Prieto/VU.